MW01124330

# MAKING GOD KNOWN

*Foundations for Evangelism*

NICO VAN ZYL

authorHOUSE®

*AuthorHouse™ UK*
*1663 Liberty Drive*
*Bloomington, IN 47403 USA*
*www.authorhouse.co.uk*
*Phone: 0800 047 8203 (Domestic TFN)*
*        +44 1908 723714 (International)*

*Published by AuthorHouse  10/07/2019*

*ISBN: 978-1-7283-9406-0 (sc)*
*ISBN: 978-1-7283-9405-3 (hc)*
*ISBN: 978-1-7283-9404-6 (e)*

*Print information available on the last page.*

*This book is printed on acid-free paper.*

# CONTENTS

# FOREWORD

The old evangelicals had a high view of God and his Word. I don't mean that all of them were Calvinists, but that they didn't worship the false god of postmodernism who cannot do anthing unless we 'speak life' or invite him into our hearts. The God of the old evangelicals was sovereign and did as he pleased. Arminians such as John Wesley believed this so that many Calvinists have a high regard for him. For instance, Calvinistic preacher Charles Spurgeon said that if two apostles had to be added to the original group, John Wesley undoubtedly would have been one of them.[1]

Calvinists and Arminians have disagreed for centuries, and yet the adherents on both sides respect men like D.L. Moody, Charles Spurgeon, and A.W. Tozer. Why is this? Is it not because these men loved God, revered his Word, had a robust biblical doctrine, and were filled with the Holy Spirit? And is it not this fact that turned these men into the powerful preachers they were?

In Foundations for Evangelism Nico van Zyl seeks to continue this legacy. He doesn't care for the fluff of modern evangelicalism. He is interested in giving us a biblical foundation for evangelism; evangelism that is founded on the solid rock of biblical doctrine. What Nico van Zyl has written agrees with the evangelism of men like John Wesley and George Whitefield. John Piper says:

---

[1] Randy Alcorn, hand in Hand (Colorado Springs: Multnomah Books, 2014), 189-190

'Unlike so much preaching today, the preaching of the eighteenth century awakening—including the evangelistic preaching of Whitefield and Wesley—was doctrinally specific and not vague. When you read the sermons of Whitefield, you are struck with how amazingly doctrinal they are.'[2]

We do not see much of this today. My heartfelt desire is that Nico van Zyl's book would succeed in bringing many preachers back to the biblical foundations for evangelism.

Ivor Jefferies
Kempton Park
October 2019

[2] John Piper, 21 Servants of Sovereign Joy (Wheaton, Illinois: Crossway, 2018), 672

# THE TEN COMMANDMENTS

**Introduction/Purposes of the law**

**The Ten Commandments**

**Conclusion**

**Bibliography and Recommended Resources**

# 1

# INTRODUCTION – THE FOUNDATIONS OF EVANGELISM

Any building that is built without a good foundation will not stand against the elements of nature. This is so especially if your house or building is built in an area where there are many natural disasters, like typhoons, or hurricanes or tornadoes or floods. These elements can wreck the building. The stronger the foundation of the building, the better the chances it has to withstand the elements.

The apostle Paul also said of his ministry to the Corinthians that he, as a master builder, laid the foundation of the spiritual house, which was none other than Jesus Christ (1 Corinthians 3:7-11). No human being can be saved from their sins and God's wrath, without having Jesus Christ as his/her Saviour and Lord. Without Jesus Christ in our lives, ruling and reigning, without Him having the pre-eminence in our lives, our spiritual lives will become a wreck.

And so it is with the work of evangelism. Without God building the house, without Him watching over us (Psalm 127:1,2), without God ruling and directing and building and strengthening the evangelist, the work will fail and all the efforts of those who evangelize will be to no avail. We do not want to work in the arm of the flesh, but in the power of the Holy Spirit. When we look at evangelism, we have to start with the foundation of evangelism, and that is God. The practice of evangelism is inconceivable without God. God is the source, the originator and the sustainer of evangelists and the work of evangelism. We as human beings did not have a good idea of how to save mankind ourselves. God is the One who planned how He would save people from their rebellion and wretchedness even before He created the universe, space and time.

In this section we are going to look at God, and secondly to the instruments he uses. Under GOD we are going to look at the sovereignty of God and His election of a people; the character of God; the Bible; the commands and promises of God; the lostness and depravity of mankind; the law of God; the gospel of God and the love of God. Without a Biblical understanding of these things we will easily fall into spiritual ditches and dangers that can wreck the work of evangelism.

Then, in the second section we are going to look at THE INSTRUMENTS GOD USES IN EVANGELISM. They are part of the foundation, because they are the means God uses to reach people with the only message that can help them.

I have included in this book another book as well as a short exposition of the Ten Commandments, because it is imperative that the Biblical evangelist be aware of the meaning of the Ten Commandments and how to use them in reaching the lost. At the end of the short exposition I have included a few gospel tracts that I have used in evangelism to show how the moral law and the presentation of the gospel converge.

My aim is that these two short books in one volume will the first part in a series on evangelism resources. The second part will be on the goals of evangelism, the third, on the need for evangelism and then part four on the practices or methods of evangelism. I pray that these truths will not leave you sitting on your couch or be complacent in the comfort of your home! This book, as with the others that I am working on, is meant to help you become an active evangelist and soul-winner, by the grace and power of God! This book will be useless unless it encourages and helps you to put on the shoes of readiness to proclaim the gospel of peace (Ephesians 6:14-15).

May we not only retreat in spiritual battle, as we should from time to time, but go on the offensive as God gives strength and the ability, actively using the Sword of the Spirit which is the Word of God!

In Christ alone,
Nico van Zyl

# 2

## THE FOUNDATIONS OF EVANGELISM (PART 1; GOD)

### 2.1 THE SOVEREIGNTY AND ELECTION OF GOD

When we talk about the sovereignty of God we mean that God is in absolute control of everything He has made. As Jesus Christ said: "not one of them (sparrows) falls to the ground apart from your Father's will " (Matthew 10:29 NKJV). Everything that happens in this world, that has happened and will happen, occurs because God ordains or permits it to happen. He can stop the birds from flying in the sky. He can stop your baby boy from crying. He makes the sun shine at the exact temperature He wants it to shine. He controls the winds (Read John 6:15-21 NKJV) and the rainfall and the droughts on this planet. Ephesians 1:11 declares: "...God works all things according to the counsel of His will" (Ephesians 1:11 NKJV). Psalms 115:3 states: "Whatever the Lord pleases He does, in heaven and in earth" (Psalm 115:3 NKJV). No one can sway His hand; no one can thwart His purposes. What He has purposed He will do. God declares, "I will accomplish all my purpose" (Isaiah 46:10 ESV). He sets up thrones and rulers and He makes them perish. 1 Samuel 2:7 states: "The Lord makes poor and makes rich. He brings low and He exalts" (1 Samuel 2:7 ESV). God declares: "See now, that I, even I, am he, and there is no God beside me; I kill and I make alive; I wound and I heal" (Deuteronomy 32:39

ESV). Every person dies at precisely the time God wants them to die: "My frame was not hidden from you, when I was being made in secret, intricately woven in the depths of the earth. Your eyes saw my unformed substance; in your book were written, every one of them, the days that were formed for me, when as yet there was none of them." (Psalm 139:15,16 ESV).

Although God rules on high, although He is involved in the smallest details of every living thing, and although no cell in the human body can function without God's sustaining hand, we are still responsible human beings and we are accountable for the lives that we live before Him. God is not the author of sin and evil and He is not responsible for the sins we are involved in. Having said this God can still stop people from sinning against Him if He so pleases. God orders everything in the world we live in exactly as He wants, yet He is not responsible for our evil motives, actions, attitudes or words. We call this the doctrine of concurrence.

If we look at the crucifixion of Jesus Christ and how He died for sinners we know that it was according to the predetermined counsel and plan of God that Jesus had to be crucified, (See Acts 2:23 NKJV) yet the Roman soldiers who crucified Him, the Jewish authorities who accused Him, Pontius Pilate who allowed it, Judas who betrayed Him, the disciples who fled and Peter who denied Him, all grievously sinned against God in the events that led to Jesus' crucifixion. And so it is with life in general. God allows many evil things to happen in this world every day. But although He can stop every sin if He so pleases, He does not do so. Because of this truth – although we cannot understand the complexity of daily living fully with our finite minds – we worship God for who He is and pray to Him that He would save those whom He has appointed to eternal life (Read Acts 13:48 ESV).

When we talk about the sovereignty of God in evangelism we believe that the work of the evangelist and the believer in Christ is not in vain (Read Isaiah 55:10 ESV; 1 Corinthians 15:58 ESV). The work that God has called every believer to do will accomplish its purpose. God has a people across the world. When they hear the gospel being preached to them the first, or second, or hundredth time, they will believe: it is the Holy Spirit who makes them alive to the truth of the Word when they are born again (See John 3:3-6 ESV). When Jesus Christ came to this earth, He came to give His life for the sheep – not for the goats (Read John 10:14-16). Jesus Christ came, "to give His life as a ransom for many" (Mark 10:45 ESV), but not for all people everywhere.

Jesus Christ did not pay the debt of all people who have ever lived. If He did that all people would go to heaven. If unbelievers don't believe in Christ they go to hell. If Jesus died for the sin of their unbelief then even the sin of not believing in Him will be forgiven. But it will not. The Bible makes it clear that those appointed to eternal life will believe and be saved (See Acts 13:48 ESV). The Bible states: "All that the Father gives me (Christ) will come to me, and whoever comes to me I will never cast out" (John 6:37 ESV). Those who come to Christ in repentance and faith will never be cast out. When Jesus prayed before He went to the cross, recorded in John 17:3-21, He prayed not for the world but for those whom the Father gave Him and those who would believe in Him by the Word of God.

God has purposed that people from every people and language, tribe and nation will be saved and be there praising the Lamb and the Father forever and ever (See Revelation 5:9;7:9 ESV). Because God secured and purchased the elect's salvation by the blood of Jesus, the appointed number will believe and God's kingdom will have no end. Isaiah 9:7 states: "Of the increase of his government and of peace there will be no end" (Isaiah 9:7 ESV). The eternal salvation of the elect of God is sure and steadfast and immovable. Jesus Christ did not only make salvation possible for humanity – He actually secured salvation for those who will believe. The sheep hear Jesus' voice; God knows His sheep and they follow Him. Jesus said "I give them eternal life, and they shall never perish; neither shall anyone snatch them out of My hand" (John 10:28 NKJV). Before the foundation of the world God chose those sheep in Christ, "to be holy and without blame before Him in love" (Ephesians 1:4 NKJV).

Because God has a people we as evangelists, Christians and missionaries can go out into the world and proclaim the gospel, knowing that those who hear and are effectually called and those who repent and believe will be forgiven their sins and be declared righteous by Christ. Because God is ruling, because God is sovereign, because God's purposes cannot be thwarted, because "all authority has been given to Christ in heaven and on earth" (Matthew 28:18 NKJV), because Christ accomplished salvation for those who will believe, because Jesus Christ conquered the grave, we can have all the confidence to go out and proclaim the glorious gospel and expect those whom God will effectually call to be saved. Romans 8:28-30 declares:

"And we know all things work together for good to those who love God, to those who are called according to His purpose. For whom He foreknew, He predestined to be conformed to the image of His Son, that He might be the firstborn among many brethren. Moreover whom He predestined these He also called; whom He called, these He also justified; and whom He justified; these He also glorified" (Romans 8:28-30 NKJV).

Romans 9 states that salvation doesn't in the final analysis depend on human effort but on God who chooses. This is not an easy thing to hear but these truths are based on Scripture (See Romans 9:13,14; Ephesians 2:8-10; Titus 3:4-7; Romans 3:24-28). The election of God and the sovereignty of God remains to a large degree a mystery to human beings. God's judgements are unsearchable and His ways are past finding out (Read Romans 11:33-36). God's glory therefore remains.

## 2.2 THE REVELATION OF GOD (HOLY SCRIPTURE)

The Word of God recorded in the Bible is our standard to distinguish truth from deception and false doctrine from true doctrine about God, humanity, salvation and sin, God's standards for right and wrong and righteousness. 2 Timothy 3:14-17 is critical in understanding why the Scriptures have been given to us. Paul the apostle is speaking to Timothy:

> "But as for you, continue in what you have learned and have firmly believed, knowing from whom you learned it and how from childhood you have been acquainted with the sacred writings, which are able to make you wise for salvation through faith in Christ Jesus. All Scripture is breathed out by God and profitable for teaching, for reproof, for correction, and for training in righteousness, that the man of God may be complete, equipped for every good work" (2 Timothy 3:14-17 ESV).

The aim of Scripture and the reason God has preserved it for the human race is so that we might know how to be saved through Jesus Christ, and to teach us concerning righteousness and how to live God-honouring lives. The Scriptures were given by the inspiration of the Holy Spirit and they are enough to teach us everything we need to know how to be saved for eternity, have eternal life in the Holy Spirit and how to live lives pleasing to God. We cannot add anything to the full revelation of God and we should never take anything away from sacred Scripture (See Revelation 22:18,19; Deuteronomy 4:2; Proverbs 30:6). "Forever, O Lord, Your word is settled in heaven" (Psalm 119:89 NKJV). No Christian commentary, systematic theology, devotional book by renowned Christian writers or any sermon preached or so-called modern-day prophecy equals or supersedes the authority of sacred Scripture. Our lives, our Christian lives, should be based on holy Scripture, because in holy Scripture we see the revelation of the character of God, His ways, His standards for truth and righteousness and the way He worked out His redemptive plan in history.

The sixty-six books we have in the Old and New Testaments have sufficient information about God, not exhaustive, but sufficient to make us wise unto salvation and to correct our sinful behaviour and attitudes, motives and words, so that we can be satisfied with God in Christ and the Holy Spirit. It is in the Bible that we find the very words of God, the unchangeable words of God that revive us, direct us, comfort us, encourage and regenerate us, warn us and guide us on the narrow way to heaven.

> "Every word of God is pure; He is a shield to those who trust in Him. Do not add to His words, lest He rebuke you, and you be found a liar" (Proverbs 30:5,6 NKJV).

> "The words of the Lord are pure words, like silver tried in a furnace of the earth, purified seven times" (Psalm 12:6 NKJV).

Because the Word of God is the chief agent in the work of regeneration by the Holy Spirit, we should *know* the Word of God, *study* the Word of God, *memorize* the Word of God and *meditate on* the Word of God, day and night (Read Psalm 1:1-4). The Word of God is the primary power in evangelism and in the proclamation of the gospel. In the Bible we find the gospel which is, "the power of God for salvation to everyone who believes" (Romans 1:16 ESV). The Bible commands us, "...take...the sword of the Spirit, which is the word of God" (Ephesians 6:17 NKJV). The Bible states that, "...the word is living and powerful." (Hebrews 4:12 NKJV) and that it is the by the word of truth by which we are born again.

> "...having been born again, not of corruptible seed but incorruptible, through the word of God which lives and abides forever, because "all flesh *is* as grass, and all the glory of man as the flower of the grass. The grass withers, and its flower falls away, But the word of the LORD endures forever." Now this is the word which by the gospel was preached to you" (I Peter 1:23-25 NKJV).

9

> "Of His own will He brought us forth by the word of truth, that we might be a kind of first fruits of His creatures." (James 1:18 NKJV).

The Word of God is our weapon that pierces the darkness. The Word of God triumphs over deception and the lies of the devil as we read it and as we proclaim it wherever we go. It gives hope to the hopeless and it convicts of sin, righteousness and judgement by the work of the Holy Spirit. By the Word of God the church is sanctified and built up in love (Read John 17:17). Without the Word of God we have no warrant to evangelize or to share the hope that is within us. It is the very foundation upon which the church is built and by God's providence we have it today preserved in thousands of manuscripts in the world and translated into hundreds of languages around the globe. By studying history we see how God has preserved it through the work of his church and the Holy Spirit. Even though we have variant readings in the thousands of manuscripts available to us we can determine with astounding precision the intent of the Holy Spirit through the pages of Scripture and the meaning of the Word of God. The variant readings of the different manuscripts available to us in Hebrew and Greek (comprising 1% of all the manuscripts) do not in the slightest vitiate or overturn the truth of Scripture, and God's plan of salvation, as well as our understanding of righteousness and what right and wrong and sin is. God has preserved so many manuscripts that we might know with certainty how He wants us to live and how we can receive eternal life through faith in Jesus Christ.

Although God used men to write the Scriptures we now have, the primary author was the Holy Spirit. God is the originator of Scripture.

> "And so we have the prophetic word confirmed, which you do well to heed as a light that shines in a dark place, until the day dawns and the morning star rises in your hearts; knowing this first, that no prophecy of Scripture is of any private interpretation, for prophecy never came by the will of man, but holy men of God spoke *as they were* moved by the Holy Spirit." (II Peter 1:19-21 NKJV).

## 2.3 THE CHARACTER OF GOD

The Holy Bible, the sixty-six books in the Old and New Testaments, reveals to us the character of God. We call it special revelation. Although God reveals aspects of His divine nature and Godhead in nature and the created order, we cannot know God savingly through natural revelation. Creation exhibits God's beauty. This can be seen in sunsets or in different flowers and animals that God has made. Creation exhibits God's power. This is seen when we hear a thunderstorm or see lighting. Animals feeding their young and birds caring and feeding their chicks demonstrate God's compassion and care for creation and living things. The complexity of the human body exhibits God's intelligence and wisdom and insight. How ecosystems work and how all the different gasses and heat and oxygen come together with many other elements to make life possible on planet earth demonstrates and reveals that God is a God of order and wisdom and power (See Romans 1:18-23).

We can talk much more about how nature reveals the divine nature of God, but the world we live in is fallen; we also see this in nature. We see things and plants and trees decaying and dying. But that was not part of the original creation. When God made the heavens and the earth in the beginning, He made it perfect and very good (See Genesis 1:27). There was no sickness, sin, death or suffering in the original creation. So when we see things dying we see God's judgement on display. Fruitful seasons and rain from heaven also reveal and display God's goodness. The stars and the galaxies in the sky reveal His greatness.

But if we look only at nature and the created order and the universe we will not enter into a personal saving relationship with God. We need another source to know God redemptively. That source is the Holy Bible. In the Bible God is revealed in various ways. He revealed Himself to the prophet Moses as follows:

> "And the LORD passed before him and proclaimed, "The LORD, the LORD God, merciful and gracious, long-suffering, and abounding in goodness and truth, keeping mercy for

thousands, forgiving iniquity and transgression and sin, by no means clearing the guilty, visiting the iniquity of the fathers upon the children and the children's children to the third and the fourth generation" (Exodus 34:6-7 NKJV).

In Nahum 1:3,4; Psalm 103:11,12; and Psalm 145:8,9 God is revealed in the same way. God is merciful and gracious, a God of truth and goodness, but also a God of justice and judgement and righteousness. In the Old Testament we see God revealed over and over again as the God that executes justice and righteousness and mercy (See Jeremiah 9:23,24; Psalm 99; Nahum, Amos etc.) God will by no means clear the guilty. He will avenge Himself on His enemies.

In Isaiah 6:1-6 God reveals Himself as the Holy One:

> "In the year that King Uzziah died, I saw the Lord sitting on a throne, high and lifted up, and the train of His robe filled the temple. Above it stood seraphim; each one had six wings: with two he covered his face, with two he covered his feet, and with two he flew. And one cried to another and said: "Holy, holy, holy is the LORD of hosts; the whole earth is full of His glory!"

> (Isaiah 6:1-3 NKJV).

God also revealed Himself as holy in Psalm 99 and in the book Isaiah as well as in many other places in the Bible. The holiness of God refers to the fact that there is no evil or unrighteousness in God. God cannot steal or lie or be deceptive or commit idolatry or dishonour His own Name. Everything God does is for the sake of His holy Name and for His glory. His glory lies not only in the fact of His holiness and purity but in all His divine attributes. God is holy and therefore He is different from us. Even the angels who are in heaven are not as holy as He is, and they who do not sin praise God for His holiness. They are only holy because God made them like that. Because of God's holiness and justice we as human beings are in a great predicament if we don't receive His forgiveness. As Psalm 130:4 says: "with you there is forgiveness that you may be feared" (Psalm 130:4 ESV). If God was not a forgiving and merciful God He wouldn't be God. All God's divine attributes combined make Him infinitely glorious.

God is not only merciful and just and righteous and wise and holy and gracious and good and forgiving and loving, which we call God's attributes that He shares (His communicable attributes) with people and angels, but He is omnipotent (All-powerful), and omniscient (All-knowing) and omnipresent (present everywhere). We call these God's transcendent attributes. The things He will never share with us to their full capacity are called His incommunicable attributes. God's transcendent and incommunicable attributes makes Him forever unique and different from us. Christians are called to be conformed to the *image* of Jesus Christ, but not to His deity. God knows everything about everyone who has ever lived. He has all the power in heaven and on earth (See Matthew 28:18-20) and He is omnipresent, and always will be. No person or angel or demon or any created being can ever hide from God. Nobody can ever keep something secret from God, and no one can ever overpower God in any way. In Psalm 139 we read the following:

> "O LORD, You have searched me and known me. You know my sitting down and my rising up; You understand my thought afar off. You comprehend my path and my lying down, And are acquainted with all my ways. For there is not a word on my tongue, But behold, O LORD, You know it altogether. You have hedged me behind and before, And laid Your hand upon me.
>
> Where can I go from Your Spirit? Or where can I flee from Your presence? If I ascend into heaven, You are there; If I make my bed in hell, behold, You are there. If I take the wings of the morning, And dwell in the uttermost parts of the sea, Even there Your hand shall lead me, And Your right hand shall hold me" (Psalms 139:1-5, 7-10 NKJV).

You might ask: How do these truths about God apply to evangelism and making God known? The revelation of God in Holy Scripture has everything to with evangelism. If we don't know who the God is whom we proclaim, how can we be effective in making Him known? I want to recommend the book: THE ATTRIBUTES OF GOD by A.W. Pink to everyone who shares the gospel with a lost and dying world. We have no business proclaiming the good news of Jesus Christ if we do not know His character. It is pivotal that we study the Word of God and be immersed in God's revelation of Himself. When we study Scripture and when we study general revelation in nature we come to know the majesty and glory and holiness and nature of God. We become familiar with the God we have offended and with the way we can be restored to His glory. Explaining the character of God should be the first thing we share with lost sinners when we attempt to evangelize them. Without a good understanding of the holiness of God, the justice of God and the wrath of God against sin, people will not accept the good news we want to bring them.

Good news is no good news unless we know the bad news of how intensely we have offended God and perceive how just the punishment and wrath are that we deserve from the Maker of the Universe. We need to understand the seriousness and sinfulness of sin and the nature of God before we evangelize and make Him known.

Another important thing that the Scriptures reveal, and that we must realize about God is that He is unchangeable in His divine perfections. God's gloriousness cannot change. God cannot become sinful or evil or unholy. There are no variables or shadow of turning with God. There is no escape from God's holiness and nature, not for anyone in all creation. We will all stand before Him one day. We will all give an account of the lives we have lived in the body (See James 1:17; Malachi 3:6; Numbers 23:19; Romans 2:14-16).

## 2.4 THE PROMISES AND COMMANDS OF GOD

There are thousands of promises that God has made to His people throughout history and they are all "*yes* and *amen*" in Christ Jesus (2 Corinthians 1:20 ESV). This means that all the promises that God has made to His people in the Old Testament and the New Testament find their ultimate fulfilment in Christ Jesus. God promised that He would crush the head of the serpent (See Genesis 3:15, the devil). This He did by Christ's perfect life, death and resurrection. God promised that all the families of the earth would be blessed through the seed of Abraham (Read Genesis 12:1-3) and God will bless them through the seed of Abraham who is Christ Jesus. God promised that when you, "trust in the Lord with all our heart and lean not on your own understanding; in all your ways acknowledge Him, He shall direct your paths" (Proverbs 3:3-5 NKJV). This He does through the Good Shepherd, Jesus Christ (Read John 10:1-5). God promised that He would write His laws within our hearts (He would give us a heart of flesh) (See Ezekiel 36:24-26) and God did that and does it and will do that before and when we repent of our sins and have faith in Jesus Christ. The new covenant is sealed by the blood of Jesus Christ and whosoever comes to Him in faith and repentance will receive the gift of the Holy Spirit and have God's laws written on their hearts.

All the promises of God in the Old and New Testament had conditions attached to them. Also, prophecies worked much the same way as the promises of God. All prophecies were also promises of God, but not all promises were prophecies. Prophecies will come to pass and have come to pass regardless of human cooperation and conditions being met. The promises of God to man always had a condition to be met. That doesn't mean the fulfilment of the promises could be achieved or merited by humans or God's people but there were always conditions attached in order that they might be fulfilled.

Let us look at two examples:

In Genesis 3:15 God promised that He would crush the head of the serpent. This would happen regardless of what humans would do. It was therefore not only a promise but a prophecy. God crushed the power of Satan through Jesus Christ.

But take the promise of Proverbs 3:3-5. There is a condition connected to this promise. If we trust in God with our whole heart and if we lean not on our understanding and if we acknowledge Him in all our ways *then* God will direct our paths. Promises like these can come to fulfilment in a person's life hundreds or thousands of times as the believer comes to Christ, but they have conditions. All the conditions in all the promises in the Bible can be summed up in turning from sin and trusting in Christ Jesus, or believing in Him.

All the promises in the Bible: "Ask and it will be given to you; seek, and you will find; knock, and it will be opened to you" (Matthew 7:7-9 ESV) must be connected to the Person and work of Jesus Christ. If we miss this we miss the whole point of why God made promises to His people.

The conditions for receiving salvation are repentance and faith in Jesus Christ (See Mark 1:15; Acts 20:21). And the summary of growing in likeness to Christ is continual repentance and faith in the Lord Jesus Christ.

When it comes to evangelism we must admit that it is based on the promises and commands of Christ. We evangelize because God has promised: "... my word...that goes out from my mouth; it shall not return to me empty, but it shall accomplish that which I purpose" (Isaiah 55:11 ESV). We evangelize and know the seed that we sow will not be in vain because God promises that the work of the Lord is not in vain:

> Therefore, my beloved brethren, be steadfast, unmovable, always abounding in the work of the Lord, since you know that your labor in the Lord is not in vain (1 Corinthians 15:58 NKJV).

> For God is not unjust so as to overlook your work and the love that you have shown for his name in serving the saints, as you still do (Hebrews 6:10 ESV).

""Behold, I am coming soon, bringing my recompense with me, to repay each one for what he has done. I am the Alpha and the Omega, the first and the last, the beginning and the end."" (Revelation 22:12-13 ESV).

Not only do we have these and other promises that our work in the Lord in evangelism will not be in vain, but we have the Lord's command to go out into all the earth and share the gospel with every person. Jesus commanded His disciples:

"Go into all the world and preach the gospel to every creature"(Mark 16:15 NKJV).

"Then said He to His servants, the wedding is ready but those who were invited were not worthy. Therefore go into the highways, and as many as you find, invite to the wedding" (Matthew 22:8,9 NKJV).

We all know that the parable of the wedding feast refers to the Marriage supper of the Lamb, Jesus Christ, and that His servants are those who should invite people from everywhere! Jesus said to His disciples:

"All authority in heaven and on earth has been given to me. Go therefore and make disciples of all nations, baptizing them in the name of the Father and of the Son and of the Holy Spirit, teaching them to observe all that I have commanded you. And behold, I am with you always, to the end of the age." (Matthew 28:18-20 ESV)

No disciple of Christ can make a disciple without evangelizing and sharing the gospel in his teaching. Disciples ought to teach the gospel in discipling. And they will be successful because God has promised to be with them unto the end of the age. God will never command something of His disciples that He doesn't give them the power to do.

And Jesus said to them, "Thus it is written, that the Christ should suffer and on the third day rise from the dead, and that repentance and forgiveness of sins should be proclaimed in his name to all nations, beginning from Jerusalem." (Luke 24:46-47 ESV).

Paul said, 'woe is me if I do not preach the gospel' (1 Corinthians 9:16 NKJV). The gospel of God, "...is the power of God to salvation for everyone who believes" (Romans 1:17,18 NKJV). The Bible declares: "For since, in the wisdom of God, the world through wisdom did not know God, it pleased God through the foolishness of the message preached to save those who believe" (1 Corinthians 1:21 NKJV). If God has chosen human beings to proclaim the gospel and if He has chosen the gospel to save people, (See 1 Peter 1:23-25) which He has, it becomes evident why we should proclaim and declare His Word to a lost and dying world. God has promised to bless His Word and He has promised to build his kingdom and church until He comes again (See Matthew 16:18).

We cannot be wiser than God and think that He will use other means to save sinners. God saves His elect through the hearing of the Word of Christ (See Romans 10:17) and He will save them as His church proclaims His gospel! Of the increase of Jesus Christ's government, peace and salvation there will be no end (Read Isaiah 9:6,7).

## 2.5 THE DEPRAVITY AND LOSTNESS OF HUMANITY

In the sixteenth century the great Reformers John Calvin, Martin Luther and others rediscovered the plight of man before God as they studied the Scriptures in the original languages. For many centuries the church of God was in the dark about their true condition before God. How depraved and lost are human beings without God? Are they partly depraved, and partially lost? Do they need some assistance to be better individuals? Do they only need assistance from God to be accepted by Him? Or are they totally depraved, and totally lost?

The Bible makes it clear in Romans 3:11-19 that humanity is unable to help itself, people are unable to save themselves. We are in fact dead in our sins and trespasses (See Ephesians 2:1-2). We don't need divine assistance only, we need to be born from above, born of the Holy Spirit. We need a new birth (Read John 3:3-5). We are radically evil and sinful. We are not as evil as we could be, not all of us! We are totally depraved, meaning there is no way we will turn to God unless the Holy Spirit makes us alive to spiritual realities. Listen to how Paul the apostle puts it:

> "as it is written: "None is righteous, no, not one; no one understands; no one seeks for God. All have turned aside; together they have become worthless; no one does good, not even one." "Their throat is an open grave; they use their tongues to deceive." "The venom of asps is under their lips." "Their mouth is full of curses and bitterness." "Their feet are swift to shed blood; in their paths are ruin and misery, and the way of peace they have not known." "There is no fear of God before their eyes."" (Romans 3:10-18 ESV).

The Scriptures here explain the condition of man without God. This passage makes it clear that we don't need improvement and self-actualization. We don't need to revamp the *self*. We need a complete change of our natures to come to God. We need spiritual regeneration. We need to be born again; we need the Holy Spirit to make us alive unto

God if we are to have any chance of coming to God and being saved. In order for us to come to Christ the Father must draw us (Read John 6:44). We are not by nature looking for or seeking after God. Rather, it is God who was and is seeking after us. Jesus came to seek and save the lost. He takes the initiative in salvation. It is God who awakens us to our sinful condition. It is God who convicts us of sin, righteousness and judgment (Read John 16:8). It is God who shows us our depravity before Him. If left to ourselves we will never seek after God. We are born in sin (Read Psalm 51:6). "We are estranged from the womb" (Psalm 58:3; ESV). We are all born in Adam with a sinful nature (Read Romans 5:11-19). We are born evil and rebellious. Again, as stated above, we are not as evil as we could be, but we are morally and totally depraved, God-hating and unable to choose God and receive His salvation unless God takes the initiative and shows us our sins and how heinous our sins are before His holy and just presence.

Many times we compare ourselves to other sinners, such as serial killers and prostitutes and thieves and murderers and rapists and say to ourselves that we are not as evil as they are. Dear reader, without God's restraining hand we will become the worst creatures of hell! Without God's restraining hand nothing will stop us from becoming as evil as Hitler or Stalin if we are given the opportunity. Many times we are not as evil as we could be because we lack the opportunity to sin in such ways. But we should not think that serial killers and rapists are more evil than the self-righteous and the religious. Was it not the Pharisees and the Scribes in Jesus' day that were excluded from the kingdom of God and tax-collectors and prostitutes that entered the kingdom of God? You see, if we start relying on our own goodness and righteousness then we are in a worse danger than when we live in spectacular sins. If we live as if we don't need God and become self-sufficient then we shut ourselves out from God's grace and mercy. This self-righteousness is what made the Pharisees of Jesus' day so contemptible in God's sight. As Charles Spurgeon said:

"The black devil of licentiousness has slain her thousands, but the white devil of self-righteousness has slain her tens of thousands."

Paul the apostle said of the Jewish leaders:

"Brothers, my heart's desire and prayer to God for them is that they may be saved. For I bear them witness that they have a zeal for God, but not according to knowledge. For, being ignorant of the righteousness of God, and seeking to establish their own, they did not submit to God's righteousness." (Romans 10:1-3 ESV).

Self-reliance is what is taking many people in our societies to hell. You are not safe at all if you think you do not need Christ desperately from day to day, hour to hour, minute to minute, and second to second. The prophet Jeremiah warned us with these words:

"The heart is deceitful above all things, and desperately sick; who can understand it? "I the Lord search the heart and test the mind, to give every man according to his ways, according to the fruit of his deeds."" (Jeremiah 17:9-10 ESV).

As the theologian John Calvin said: "the heart of man is an idol factory." Left with an unregenerate heart no human can image what we are capable of. And relying on our own abilities and living independently before God may be the worst kind of evil. It is a heinous crime against God's majesty to inwardly say to Him: "I don't need you." What surprise God-haters and God-ignorers and God-deniers will face when they stand before God one day face to face and hear the words: "depart from me, you workers of lawlessness" (Matthew 7:23 ESV).

Jesus Christ described the heart of man in this way:

"Do you not see that whatever goes into a person from outside cannot defile him, since it enters not his heart but his stomach, and is expelled?" (Thus he declared all foods clean.) And he said,

"What comes out of a person is what defiles him. For from within, out of the heart of man, come evil thoughts, sexual immorality, theft, murder, adultery, coveting, wickedness, deceit, sensuality, envy, slander, pride, foolishness. All these evil things come from within, and they defile a person."" (Mark 7:18-23 ESV).

We are eternally lost, eternally damned, eternally wicked and totally depraved left to ourselves and our own devices. We are without hope and salvation without God shining into our hearts the truth of the gospel. If we want to know the extent of our depravity before God all we have to do is to look at the law of God and the Ten Commandments. In the law of God we see our guilt to the fullest extent. In God's moral law we see how many times we have fallen short of the perfection and glory of God.

## 2.6 THE LAW AND JUDGEMENT OF GOD

The best way to know our own lostness and depravity before God is to look deeply into the law of God and especially the Ten Commandments. By the law of God I mean the first five books of the Bible (The Torah): Genesis, Exodus, Leviticus, Numbers and Deuteronomy. The law of God can be divided into the ceremonial law, the moral law and the civic law. The ceremonial law in the Torah had to do with the construction of the Tabernacle, the Temple service, the animal sacrifices and dietary laws that God instituted for the nation of Israel. These ceremonial laws were only temporary and were a shadow of the things to come in Jesus Christ. All the animal sacrifices in the Old Testament pointed to Jesus Christ and His sacrifice that would take away the sins of the world (Read John 1:29). With the coming of Jesus Christ, who was the substance of the things to come (See Colossians 2:14-16), God fulfilled the ceremonial laws of old Israel (Read Matthew 5:17-18) and abrogated them. That is why the curtain in the temple was torn in two when Jesus died on the cross (Read Matthew 27:51).

The civic law that God instituted was meant for the nation of Israel and when that nation was judged in 67AD the civic law lost its function because the Everlasting King and eternal Judge came into the world. The civic law with its many commandments had benefit for the Israelites, and children of God can still make use of them and obtain principles that would benefit societies and cultures today. But as binding on the people of God today they should not always be applied in every circumstance. For example, we as children of God don't have to rest from all work after every six years and every 49 years. We don't have to celebrate the yearly feasts the Israelites used to celebrate. But we should honour the principle for work and rest and celebrate the salvivic events in history wrought by God (the birth of Christ, the death of Christ, the resurrection, the Ascension of Christ and the day of Pentecost). We are not forbidden to wear clothes of different material (Deuteronomy 22:9) but we are to obey the principle of separating from worldliness and not mixing idolatry with godliness and so on. In other words, the moral law embedded in the civic law guides us as Christians even today.

What is especially of concern to us at this stage in evangelism is the moral law of God, given to us especially in the Ten Commandments and its out-workings in the Torah (Read Leviticus 18:1-23). The law of God shows us the nature of sin. It shows us the *sinfulness* of sin. "The law of God is holy, and the commandment is holy righteous and good" (Romans 7:7 ESV) and is also the expression of God's character. In the Ten Commandments we see what God loves and what God hates. We see in them what God condemns and what God commands. We see what behaviour He blesses and what behaviour He curses (Read Deuteronomy 27,28). Although the Ten Commandments are given in the negative "you shall not murder" (Exodus 20:13 ESV), it doesn't mean the positive is not required: to protect innocent life and those who are vulnerable, or "you shall have no gods before Me" (Exodus 20:3 ESV), "You shall love the Lord your God with all your heart and with all your soul and with all your mind" (Matthew 22:37 ESV) etc.

What is especially important for us in the law of God and the Ten Commandments is that it shows us how we have offended God. Each of the Ten Commandments represents a family of sins. For example "you shall not murder" (Exodus 20:13 ESV), prohibits taking an innocent life, abortion, euthanasia, hatred towards a person, envy, jealousy, unrighteous anger etc. "You shall not commit adultery" (Exodus 20:14 ESV), prohibits "sexual lust, fornication, incest, paedophilia, bestiality, homosexuality etc. If we look deeply into the law of God we would see how many times we have offended God's majesty and infinite worth and realize we deserve punishment from God. In the Ten Commandments and in the Torah we see that God never clears the guilty (Read Exodus 34:4-6; 20:4-9) and that, because of our sins, we deserve an infinite punishment. We deserve infinite punishment, everlasting hell, because we have sinned against an Infinitely holy God. If God was not as valuable and worthy and glorious as He is then our sentence would not be unlimited and deserving of eternal hell. Since God is infinite and almighty and the Creator and Sustainer of everything we deserve such an infinite and severe sentence.

We see that sin is serious in the narrative of Adam and Eve. God said they would surely die when they ate of the tree in the middle of the garden and they did die when they ate (Read Genesis 2:10-3:15). They spiritually died when they sinned and their sin has been affecting the human race ever since. Adam was the Federal head, the representation of mankind in the beginning when God made the heavens and earth and because of his sin we all became sinners (See Romans 5:12-21). "For as in Adam all die" (1 Corinthians 15:22 ESV). Adam also eventually died and all humans will die physically as a result of sin.

We also see in the Torah the veracity of sin and the judgment of God on sin. This is most clearly seen in the narrative of Noah in Genesis 6. Because "every intention of the thoughts of his heart was only evil continually" (Genesis 6:5 ESV) God decided to destroy mankind, except for Noah, his family and selected animals and life-forms. God punished mankind for their sins with death. God never can just sweep our sins under a rug and forgive. Because He is just there must be punishment for sin. There must be divine payment for every sin. That is so because we reject God's authority over us when we sin, we despise His rightful ownership over us, and we insult His worthiness and value. Every time we sin we say, in fact, "God, we choose sin instead of you. We would rather have sin than you. We would rather be satisfied with sin than with you." And because God is infinitely valuable and worthy and just and holy we deserve an infinitely worthy sentence. The sentence against each of our sins is death: spiritual death and physical death. Death came into the world by one man, Adam; everlasting life came into the world through Jesus Christ (Read Romans 5:12-22). "The soul who sins shall die" (Ezekiel 18:20 ESV). "The wages of sin is death" (Romans 6:23 ESV). "...for in the day that you eat of of it you shall surely die" (Genesis 2:17 ESV). Genesis 2 relates the story of the tree of good and evil. God said they must never eat of that tree.

Because we were made in the image of God (Genesis 1:27) we have moral motions. We are moral beings. That means we can differentiate between evil and good, between right and wrong. We are like God in that respect. But because we are born in sin and because we have *all* violated God's standards for us, encapsulated in the Ten Commandments, we deserve punishment from God. We are all guilty before God. The world will face judgment before God. We will give an account before God of how we have lived (Read Romans 2:14-16).

> "Then I saw a great white throne and Him who sat on it, from whose face the earth and the heaven fled away. And there was found no place for them. And I saw the dead, small and great, standing before God, and books were opened. And another book was opened, which is the Book of Life. And the dead were judged according to their works, by the things which were written in the books. The sea gave up the dead who were in it, and Death and Hades delivered up the dead who were in them. And they were judged, each one according to his works. Then Death and Hades were cast into the lake of fire. This is the second death. And anyone not found written in the Book of Life was cast into the lake of fire." (Revelation 20:11-15 NKJV)

The Old Testament is an account of how God judged individuals and the nations for their sins. God used the Philistines, the Syrians, the Assyrian Empire and the Babylonian Empires to judge His people. And God has done that throughout history. Even if people have never heard the law of God or the Ten Commandments they will face judgment because God has written His laws on our hearts and He has revealed His eternal power and His divinity in the things that He made, in nature and creation (See Romans 1:18-24). We are all without excuse before God because we have rejected Him and rebelled against the light of nature and of God in our conscience. Our guilt is real because it is moral. By nature we reject God's love and God's goodness because we love evil. We cannot save ourselves from our sins. We cannot do what we ought to do: obey God's laws. But we do what we want to do: sin. And because we do what we want to do, sin, we are accountable to God and guilty before Him for every sin we commit.

As evangelists we can only be successful and do what God wants us to do if we first declare the law of God and the demands of the law and show our hearers how they fall short of God's standards and His glory before we give them the good news of the gospel. We have to give our hearers the bad news first before they will ever receive the good news of the gospel of Jesus Christ. If people are not aware of how they have offended God and broken His holy laws and grieved His Holy Spirit and what punishment and judgment they deserve, why should they care for the good news of salvation? If we don't tell people how sick they really are why would they want spiritual healing, salvation?

In the Old Testament we see how the prophets always declared the sins of the people and the judgements of God before they gave them the hope of the gospel and the hope of forgiveness if they would repent of their sins. Evangelists that reject this order will breed a bunch of false converts that only want Jesus for their own end or for the gifts of love, peace and joy and forgiveness that He may give them.

If we don't see our own danger before we see the remedy we won't come to God for the right reasons. The evangelist Ray Comfort has shown us clearly why it is so important to use the law of God in evangelism to convict the sinner of his sins and show him the nature of sin. We must tell people to flee from the wrath to come (Read 1 Thessalonians 1:10). This was also the method great preachers used in past centuries:

The purpose of the law is firstly to strip us of our pride and our own righteousness.

Charles Spurgeon said, "they will never accept grace until they tremble before a just and holy law."

And Martin Luther said, "the first duty of the gospel preacher is to declare God's law and show the nature of sin."

Romans 7:7 states, "I would not have known coveteousness unless the law had said 'you shall not covet'" (Romans 7:7).

The apostle Paul made it clear how to use the law of God lawfully, that is, to convict the sinner of his sin:

> "But we know that the law is good if one uses it lawfully, knowing this: that the law is not made for a righteous person, but for the lawless and insubordinate, for the ungodly and for sinners, for the unholy and profane, for murderers of fathers and murderers of mothers, for manslayers, for fornicators, for sodomites, for kidnappers, for liars, for perjurers, and if there is any other thing that is contrary to sound doctrine, according to the glorious gospel of the blessed God which was committed to my trust."(I Timothy 1:8-11 NKJV).

We use the law of God lawfully if we use it as Jesus Christ did when He encountered the rich young ruler. Jesus used the law of God to convict the rich young ruler of his sins. When the self-righteous young ruler justified himself, Jesus pointed to his riches as his idol.

> "A man ran up and knelt before him and asked him, "Good Teacher, what must I do to inherit eternal life?" And Jesus said to him, "Why do you call me good? No one is good except God alone. You know the commandments: 'Do not murder, Do not commit adultery, Do not steal, Do not bear false witness, Do not defraud, Honor your father and mother.'" And he said to him, "Teacher, all these I have kept from my youth." And Jesus, looking at him, loved him, and said to him, "You lack one thing: go, sell all that you have and give to the poor, and you will have treasure in heaven; and come, follow me." (Mark 10:17-21 ESV).

We will be wise if we also use the law of God to show people their sins. And after we have done so, we give them the remedy, the cure. In our gospel presentation we must first diagnose the sick with their spiritual cancer before we can prescribe the cure: the gospel! For self-righteous people we should use the law. For the contrite of heart, the broken and those desperate for salvation, we give the gospel.

## 2.7 THE GOSPEL OF GOD

While Jesus Christ was on this earth, He began His public ministry with the words: "The time is fulfilled, and the kingdom of God is at hand; repent and believe in the gospel" (Mark 1:15 ESV). When Paul wrote his letter to the Christians in Rome, he said the following:

> "For I am not ashamed of the gospel, for it is the power of God for salvation to everyone who believes, to the Jew first and also to the Greek. For in it the righteousness of God is revealed from faith for faith, as it is written, "The righteous shall live by faith."" (Romans 1:16-17 ESV)

The word *gospel* means "good news" and in the context of the Bible it means "the good news of God to the world." You will not see the good news of God as good at all unless you know of the plight of your soul before God. We have a great need before God. We sinned against God and we stand guilty before Him. Our natures are corrupt. We have wicked hearts. We have done evil and therefore we deserve God's judgement. We deserve to go to hell because we are evil and stand guilty before God.

Before people will appreciate the gospel, they have to see their desperate need for a Saviour!

The first four books of the New Testament, *Matthew, Mark, Luke* and *John,* are called the four gospels. They are orderly accounts of the birth, life, death and resurrection of Jesus Christ and what He did and said while He lived on this earth. We can say that they give us different angles or portraits of the truth of Jesus Christ. Just as four different painters who draw the same landscape or mountain would capture different truths about the particular mountain or landscape, so each writer of the four gospels captured different truths and put different emphases on the Person and work of Jesus Christ. All four gospels reveal truth about Jesus Christ, His Person and His work on earth. The gospel deals with the Person and Work of Jesus Christ. The gospel deals with redemption accomplished through Christ and redemption applied through Christ and the Holy Spirit.

In the letters of Paul in the New Testament we get a clearer focus on the meaning of the life, death and resurrection of Jesus Christ. Some Biblical scholars differentiate between the gospel of the kingdom and the gospel of salvation in the New Testament and in the letters of Paul. The gospel of the kingdom they say deals with the rule and authority of Jesus Christ and the gospel of salvation deals with how God saves people from their sins. I will not differentiate between these two gospels, but treat them as one, because both of these themes in the Bible come together in the Person and Work of Jesus Christ.

The Bible makes it clear that it is the gospel that is "the power of God unto salvation for everyone who believes" (Romans 1:16 ESV). It is through the Word of God, the gospel being preached (See 1 Corinthians 1:21), which is the Word of truth, that people are saved from their sins and are born again by the Holy Spirit. People cannot be saved from the wrath of God and from their sins by mere education or doing good works or being baptized or by just confessing their sins to God. There needs to be a power encounter with God in the Holy Spirit whereby people hear the truth of the gospel and believe it. I will elaborate on this truth later. Peter the apostle said:

> "since you have been born again, not of perishable seed but of imperishable, through the living and abiding word of God; for "All flesh is like grass and all its glory like the flower of grass. The grass withers, and the flower falls, but the word of the Lord remains forever." And this word is the *good news* that was preached to you" (1 Peter 1:23-25 ESV).

**Here is a Biblical definition of the gospel of God:**

1) God sent His only begotten Son, Jesus Christ, who is God Himself, into this world. He sent Him to Israel, as prophesied in the Scriptures, about 2000 years ago.

2) He was miraculously conceived of the Holy Spirit, by Mary, His earthly mother.

3) Jesus Christ was and is God in the flesh, in human form. He was also truly a human being who got tired and hungry as all humans do. He had a real human nature.

4) He lived a blameless, sinless life, fulfilled the righteousness of the law on behalf of His people, and exhibited the righteousness and nature of God in a perfect way.

5) He died a substitutionary death on behalf of His people, satisfied the justice of God (the just requirement of the law), absorbed and set aside the wrath of God on behalf His people.

6) After three days He physically rose from the dead and thereby conquered the power of death, Satan, sin and sinful human nature. God vindicated Jesus Christ by raising Him from the dead by the power of the Holy Spirit and declared Him to be the Son of God.

7) After 40 days, after His resurrection, Jesus ascended to heaven and was seated at the right hand of the Father while all authority in heaven and earth has been given unto Him.

8) Everyone who repents of his/her sins and believes in the Person of Jesus Christ and His substitutionary death (finished work), receiving Him as Lord and Saviour and Righteousness, will be reconciled to God,

9) will be given the Holy Spirit as an everlasting gift, will receive eternal life, justification, forgiveness of sins, life-long sanctification in the Holy Spirit, an inheritance in heaven, will be adopted as God's son or daughter and be glorified with a new body once Christ returns.

I want to summarize the gospel as the *accomplishment* of redemption in Christ and the *application* of redemption in Christ. The gospel involves both of these realities. The gospel is essentially not good unless it is applied to the elect, those who believe and repent of their sins. We can also say that the gospel is not good until each believer is eternally glorified, because that is the reason Christ came, to save us from the guilt, power and presence of sin. Full salvation will only happen in heaven.

Let us unpack this definition point by point:

**1)God sent His only begotten Son, Jesus Christ, who is God Himself, into this world. He sent Him to Israel, as prophesied in the Scriptures, about 2000 years ago.**

We see this truth very clearly in the gospel of John. Jesus Christ is the only begotten Son of God sent into this world. Jesus Christ never had a beginning. He is Everlasting. "In the beginning was the Word, and the Word was with God, and the Word was God … and the Word became flesh and dwelt among us, ..." (John 1:1-3;14 ESV). The letter to the Hebrews makes it very clear that Jesus Christ is God, "…the radiance of the glory of God and the exact imprint of his nature" (Hebrews 1:3 ESV). Christians believe in the Trinity, Father, Son and Holy Spirit eternally existing in three Persons, equal in essence and nature but having different roles. The fact that Jesus is called the Son of God doesn't mean that there was physical sex with Mary His earthly mother and God. That concept would be blasphemous. God is Spirit and cannot have sex with humans. He is holy. Jesus Christ is called the only Begotten Son of God the Father, meaning He has a special relationship with the Father that born again children don't have and cannot have, as He is God. God sent Christ into this world in history to Israel. The fact that Jesus would come to the world and what He would do, were prophesied in the Scriptures given by God to His people over many centuries. The people of God expected the Messiah to come. Jesus fulfilled more than three hundred prophecies in His life, death and resurrection. We call Jesus's becoming a human, the incarnation of God. It is important to realize that Jesus was the Only Begotten of the Father, there were not many incarnations of God in history (Read Hebrews 9:22-28), there was only one. He came in the fullness of time.

## 2) He was miraculously conceived of the Holy Spirit in Mary His earthly mother

The Bible makes it clear that the birth of Jesus Christ was a miracle (Read Matthew 1:18-25). It cannot be repeated by a human being or through experimentation. He was conceived by the Holy Spirit (Read Luke 1:26-80). Jesus was called Emmanuel, which means God with us, to fulfil the prophecy in Isaiah 7:14. He was born of God, without sexual union. Mary was a virgin.

> "In the sixth month the angel Gabriel was sent from God to a city of Galilee named Nazareth, to a virgin betrothed to a man whose name was Joseph, of the house of David. And the virgin's name was Mary…..And the angel said to her, "Do not be afraid, Mary, for you have found favour with God. And behold, you will conceive in your womb and bear a son, and you shall call his name Jesus. He will be great and will be called the Son of the Most High. And the Lord God will give to him the throne of his father David, and he will reign over the house of Jacob forever, and of his kingdom there will be no end." And Mary said to the angel, "How will this be, since I am a virgin?" And the angel answered her, "The Holy Spirit will come upon you, and the power of the Most High will overshadow you; therefore the child to be born will be called holy—the Son of God." (Luke 1:26-27, 30-35 ESV).

## 3) Jesus Christ was and is God in the flesh, in human form. He was also truly a human being who got tired and hungry as all humans do. He had a real human nature.

Some people in history have tried to show that Jesus was not really a human but was like a spirit in the form of a human. The Bible makes it very clear, however, that Jesus was really a human. He slept and ate and got tired and cried and worked with His hands as a carpenter before His public ministry. The book of Hebrews goes so far as to say that Jesus never sinned:

"Seeing then that we have a great High Priest who has passed through the heavens, Jesus the Son of God, let us hold fast our confession. For we do not have a High Priest who cannot sympathize with our weaknesses, but was in all points tempted as we are, yet without sin." (Hebrews 4:14-15 NKJV)

**4) He lived a blameless, sinless life, fulfilled the righteousness of the law on behalf of his people, and exhibited the righteousness and nature of God in a perfect way.**

A few times in the Scriptures the Bible makes it clear that Jesus Christ never sinned. He never sinned in thought, word, action, and attitude or in His disposition. He lived a perfect life and so obtained a perfect righteousness. That is one of the reasons why God came to earth, to live the life we could never live and to become a perfect Saviour for us. If Jesus had sinned once in His life, if He ever made one mistake He wouldn't be able to save us from our sins, because then He would also need a Saviour to save Him from His sins. We know that the punishment of sin is death (Read Romans 6:23). If Jesus had ever sinned once then He had to die for His own sins.

"For to this you have been called, because Christ also suffered for you, leaving you an example, so that you might follow in his steps. He **committed no sin,** neither was deceit found in his mouth. When he was reviled, he did not revile in return; when he suffered, he did not threaten, but continued entrusting himself to him who judges justly" (1 Peter 2:21-23 ESV).

"For our sake he made him to be sin who **knew no sin**, so that in him we might become the righteousness of God" (2 Corinthians 5:21 ESV).

"For we do not have a high priest who is unable to sympathize with our weaknesses, but one who in every respect has been tempted as we are, **yet without sin**" (Hebrews 4:15 ESV).

Jesus came to obey all the laws of the Old Testament in a perfect way. He came to satisfy the just requirements of the law so that He can justify us. Jesus did not only die in our place as a substitute but He also lived a perfect life as our substitute so that by faith in Him we can stand perfect before God. Jesus Christ came to live a perfect life on our behalf so that through Him we can be accepted by God. When we are in union with Christ, God doesn't look at us through the things we have done, but through the merits and achievements of Christ. The whole of Jesus' life was a life of perfection. Jesus Christ exhibited the perfect divine nature of God in all that He did. Not only did the hundreds of miracles of Jesus exhibit the compassion and love of God in a perfect way but also God's holiness and His hatred for sin and for sinful hypocrites. We see the full panorama of God's perfections shine through and on display through the life of Christ Jesus. And God reckons Christ's righteousness to us when we trust in Him. The righteousness of Christ accounted to the believer becomes the ground of our justification before God. Without that righteousness accounted to us by faith no one will see God!

> "For God has done what the law, weakened by the flesh, could not do. By sending his own Son in the likeness of sinful flesh and for sin, he condemned sin in the flesh, in order that the righteous requirement of the law might be fulfilled in us, who walk not according to the flesh but according to the Spirit." (Romans 8:3-4 ESV).

**5) He died a substitutionary death on behalf of His people, satisfied the justice of God (the just requirement of the law), and absorbed and set aside the wrath of God on behalf His people.**

Jesus Christ came to "save His people from their sins" (Matthew 1:21 ESV) He did not die for His own sins, because He was sinless. He died for the sins of His people. He laid down His life for His sheep (Read John 10:15). He gave, "...his life as a ransom for many" (Mark 10:45 ESV). He was the Lamb of God, "...who takes away the sin of the world" (John 1:29 ESV). He came to reconcile the world unto Himself (Read 2

Corinthians 5:17-19). He did not only die for His people among the Jews but for the whole world. The world in these passages means that God has a people across the world, in every nation, and tribe and language group and ethnicity (See Revelation 5:9; 7:9). Jesus didn't pay for every sin of every man that has ever lived. If that be the case then every person would go to heaven, because then the sin of unbelief, of not believing in Jesus, would also be forgiven. <u>But the Bible makes it clear that He bore the sins of His people on the cross. He did not only make salvation and forgiveness of sins possible, He actually paid for the sins of His elect across the world. He actually purchased eternal salvation for His people.</u> With His own blood being spilled He purchased faith and repentance as well for those who He would draw to Himself.

The Bible says that "without the shedding of blood there is no forgiveness of sins" (Hebrews 9:22 ESV). That is why Jesus had to die. The punishment of sin is death (Read Romans 6:23). "The soul who sins shall die" (Ezekiel 18:20 ESV). <u>Because Jesus never sinned and because He was God His death could atone for the sins of believers</u>. The punishment we deserve is infinite and unlimited. But Jesus Christ was God; only He could absorb and set aside the anger of God because He was and is the infinite worthy and valuable God. No one else could atone for our sins, no one else was able to absorb the unlimited wrath of God. No one else could, because all have sinned and have fallen under God's judgement. We were all separated from the glory of God. Jesus satisfied the justice of God, because He was God who obeyed the law perfectly and obtained a perfect experiential obedience to the law. He died as a substitute and fulfilled all the animal sacrifices given as requirements in the old covenant on that cross. It is written: "Christ redeemed us from the curse of the law by becoming a curse for us" (Galatians 3:13 ESV). He was the propitiation for the sins of His people (See 1 John 2:2; 4:10).

### ***Jesus Christ came to save us from God, (His wrath against sin) by God (the Holy Spirit) for God (His glory) and in God (the Holy Spirit).***

When Jesus cried out the words, "it is finished" (John 19:30 ESV) it meant that He did everything necessary to reconcile us to God. Jesus was abandoned by His Father, in his human nature, on the cross, so that we can be accepted. He was rejected so that we can be adopted into His family. He was cursed on our behalf so that we can be eternally blessed in the Holy Spirit!

> "for all have sinned and fall short of the glory of God, and are justified by his grace as a gift, through the redemption that is in Christ Jesus, whom God put forward as a propitiation by his blood, to be received by faith. This was to show God's righteousness, because in his divine forbearance he had passed over former sins. It was to show his righteousness at the present time, so that he might be just and the justifier of the one who has faith in Jesus." (Romans 3:23-26 ESV).

> **6) After three days He physically rose from the dead and thereby conquered the power of death, Satan, sin and sinful human nature. God vindicated Jesus Christ by raising Him from the dead by the power of the Holy Spirit and declared Him to be the Son of God.**

The Bible makes it very clear that God raised Jesus Christ from the dead by the power of the Holy Spirit and the glory of the Father (Read Ephesians 1:18-20; Romans 8:9-11; Romans 6:4). The fact that God raised Jesus from the dead in a glorified body proved that God accepted His sacrifice and that He was the only Begotten Son of God (Read Romans 1:4). Because Jesus never sinned death could not hold Him in the grave. He didn't die for His own sin, but for the sin of His people, His elect people. All the gospels make it clear that there were eyewitnesses who saw Jesus in a glorified body (See John 21:1-10; Matthew 28:1-11; Luke 24:1-10; Mark 16:1-10). Paul the apostle said that if we don't believe that Jesus Christ rose physically from the dead in a spiritual, incorruptible body, our faith is worthless and that we are still in our sins (Read 1 Corinthians 15:11-21). Sin came into the world through Adam, the first representative of mankind. Through the last or second Adam, Jesus Christ, the second representation of humanity, comes eternal life, forgiveness of sins and victory over death and sin (See Romans

5:12-21). Jesus conquered Satan on the cross because He never gave in to sin when tempted. He broke the power of sin, because He is God who never sinned, and He broke the power of death, because He died a substitutionary death and because He absorbed and set aside the coming wrath of God against sin, for those who believe.

> "Inasmuch then as the children have partaken of flesh and blood, He Himself likewise shared in the same, that through death He might destroy him who had the power of death, that is, the devil, and release those who through fear of death were all their lifetime subject to bondage" (Hebrews 2:14-15 NKJV).

> "having wiped out the handwriting of requirements that was against us, which was contrary to us. And He has taken it out of the way, having nailed it to the cross. Having disarmed principalities and powers, He made a public spectacle of them, triumphing over them in it." (Colossians 2:14-15 NKJV)

In Adam we all died but through Jesus Christ we will all be made alive (Read 1 Corinthians 5:22). Adam catapulted the human race into misery, death and the slavery of sins, but through Jesus Christ believers will have eternal life, hope and joy.

**7) After forty days after His death Jesus ascended to heaven and was seated at the right hand of the Father while all authority in heaven and earth has been given unto Him**

All authority in heaven and on earth has been given unto Jesus Christ (See Matthew 28:18). Jesus ascended into heaven on a cloud (Read Acts 1:11). He is seated at the right hand of the Father and all principalities and powers and angels and every name that can be named in this world and in the next is submitted unto His authority (See Ephesians 1:20-22; Philippians 2:5-11). All judgment has been given unto Jesus Christ (Read John 5:22). He will judge the living and the dead from all ages to come (Read Revelation 20:10-15). He is now the King of kings and the Lord of lords. Nothing and no one has more power than Him. Every knee will one day bow and declare that He is Lord and King even if they now refuse to do so. Because of His work of salvation He has this position in the universe. It is not a question of accepting Him as Lord but of *submitting* to Him as the Lord of your life. He is Lord and King over all peoples and Angels and Demons. It is a case of submitting and subjecting oneself to his supreme authority, willingly or unwillingly.

**8) Everyone who repents of his sins and believes in the Person of Jesus Christ and His substitutionary death (finished work), receiving Him as Lord and Saviour and Righteousness, will be reconciled to God**.

Although God has reconciled His people to Himself, the recipients of His grace don't receive it automatically. We are commanded to repent of our sins and believe in Jesus Christ in order to receive His salvation. Salvation is a free gift to be received by faith (Read Ephesians 2:8,9; Titus 3:4-6; Romans 3:24-26; Romans 6:23). Everyone who receives Christ, and believes in Him will be saved. It is written: "But as many as received Him, to them He gave the right to become children of God, to those who believe in His name" (John 1:12 NKJV). But we receive this gift by biblical repentance and faith in Jesus Christ. We cannot have saving faith without biblical repentance. You cannot believe savingly without turning to Jesus Christ. If your eyes are fixed on the things of this world and the pleasures of sin and self-righteousness you will not be able to see the glory of Christ. Biblical repentance involves a change of heart (contrition and hatred for sin) a change of mind (conviction), admission of your guilt (confession) and a change of behaviour (conversion). Unless the Holy Spirit makes you aware of your sins, unless the Holy Spirit makes you alive (See Ephesians 2.1-5) and unless you subsequently confess your sins to God and be broken-hearted about them (See Psalm 34:18; Psalm 51:17), you will not be able to see the preciousness and worth of God. Biblical repentance (Read 2 Timothy 2:20) and genuine faith in Christ are gifts given by God through Jesus Christ and were purchased by the blood of Christ. If we repent in a biblical way and believe in Christ, it will be the work of God, although we are not passive in this process. We are involved in repentance and faith in Jesus. It is not our repentance and faith that saves us from the wrath of God and our sins, but it is Christ who saves us. We should never make faith meritorious. Repentance and faith are just the channels that connect us to the supreme Treasure, Lord and Saviour, who is Jesus Christ. It is Christ alone who saves in the Holy Spirit (Read Acts 4:12; 1 John 5:12).

We have to receive Christ as our Lord and Saviour and Righteousness to be saved from our sins. We cannot think we only want Jesus to save us from our sins but not want Him to be our Ruler and King. If we don't submit to Him as Ruler of our lives, then we have a Christ of our own imagination. We have to receive Christ for who He is, Lord, Saviour and our Treasure of righteousness. We have to receive Christ as God.

The gospel of God is not good news unless it actually reconciles us to God. In His book, "God is the Gospel" John Piper makes it clear that all the benefits of the gospel, namely forgiveness of sins, deliverance from sins, escape from hell, an inheritance in heaven, peace of mind etc. wouldn't be good unless they bring us into fellowship with God in the Holy Spirit (Read 1 John 1:4-7; 1 Peter 3:18). This is a very important aspect of the gospel. Many people want all the benefits of the gospel but they don't want God! They don't love the beauty and glory and being of Christ. They don't love and esteem the holiness of God. They don't want to be inconvenienced and suffer for the gospel. They only want the blessings of God but not the being of a holy God in their lives. If God does not reconcile us to Himself and if we don't receive the Holy Spirit as an abiding reality in us, making His home within us, then Jesus's suffering and dying on the cross will have been senseless and useless.

**9) We will be given the Holy Spirit as an everlasting gift, will receive eternal life, justification, forgiveness of sins, life-long sanctification in the Holy Spirit, an inheritance in heaven; we will be adopted as God's son or daughter and be glorified with a new body once Christ returns.**

With receiving Christ in your life, you receive all the spiritual blessings in heavenly places which include: the fullness of the Holy Spirit, justification, forgiveness of sins, deliverance from your sins and the power of Satan, an inheritance in heaven and many others to come in the new heavens and the new earth. By faith in Jesus Christ we are declared righteous in God's sight and are therefore justified in God's courtroom. If God did not spare His only begotten Son but gave Him for us all will He not give us all things beneficial, which also includes suffering and tribulation that would make us conformed to Christ's image? (Read Romans 8:32-37). With the Holy Spirit within us the love of God is poured out into our hearts (Read Romans 5:5). It is written: "Eye has not seen, nor ear heard, nor have entered into the heart of man the things which God has prepared for those who love Him" 1 Corinthians 2:9 NKJV). With receiving Christ as your brother and Saviour and Lord, and the Holy Spirit, you are adopted as God's child (Read Romans 8:16; Galatians 4:3-9). Having Christ and the Holy Spirit in your life you become part of the family of God.

> "For you did not receive the spirit of slavery to fall back into fear, but you have received the Spirit of adoption as sons, by whom we cry, "Abba! Father!" The Spirit himself bears witness with our spirit that we are children of God, and if children, then heirs—heirs of God and fellow heirs with Christ, provided we suffer with him in order that we may also be glorified with him" (Romans 8:15-17 ESV).

God promises that the good work He starts in the believer, He will complete (Read Philipians 1:6). If God justified you, you will be sanctified and eventually be glorified (See Romans 9:30). God promises that those who believe in Christ will have eternal life (Read John 3.16) and that means God will purify you and sanctify you throughout your life until He glorifies you with an incorruptible body. What God starts, He will finish! These spiritual blessings we receive from God is called the application of redemption. Christ and the Holy Spirit applies this salvation. This is part of the gospel, the gospel of grace.

**This gospel is the power of God unto salvation for everyone who believes!**

**Resources:**
1. Piper, J. (2011). God is the Gospel. Crossway.
2. Piper. J. (2007). The Future of Justifcation. Crossway.
3. Keller. T. (2012). Center Church. Zondervan.
4. Sproul. R.C. (1992). Essential Truths of the Christian Faith. Tyndale.
5. Sproul. R.C. (2017). How can I be right with God? Reformation Trust.
6. Dever. M. (2013). Nine Marks of a Healthy Church. Crossway.
7. Murray. J. (2015). Redemption Accomplished and Applied. Eerdmans.
8. Kennedy. D.J. (1980). Why I believe. Word Publishing.

## 2.8 THE LOVE OF GOD

The love of God is not just a fluffy, warm feeling. It is revealed in a Person, the God-Man – Christ Jesus. According to the theologian Wayne Grudem, the love of God means that God eternally gives of Himself to others and continues to give Himself to those who believe.

The love of God is one of the great themes of Scripture: Here are a few Scripture verses to show us that the love of God is CENTRAL to God's redemptive plan revealed in the Bible: this is however not an exhaustive list:

It is written: "How precious is your lovingkindness, O God! Therefore the children of men put their trust in the shadow of Your wings" (Psalm 36:7 NKJV).

It is written: "For as high as the heavens are above the earth, so great is his steadfast love toward those who fear him" (Psalm 103:11 ESV)

"But the steadfast love of the Lord is from everlasting to everlasting on those who fear him, and his righteousness to children's children" (Psalm 103:17 ESV).

Jeremiah 31:3 states: "The LORD has appeared of old to me, *saying*: "Yes, I have loved you with an everlasting love; Therefore with lovingkindness I have drawn you" (Jeremiah 31:3 NKJV).

The most famous verse in the Bible states: "For God so loved the world that He gave His only begotten Son, that whosoever believes in Him should not perish but everlasting life" (John 3:16 NKJV).

John 13:1 reveals: "when Jesus knew that His hour had come that He should depart from this world to the Father, having loved His own who were in the world, He loved them to the end" (John 13:1 NKJV).

Ephesians 2:4,5 states about the believers: "But God, who is rich in mercy, because of His great love with which He loved us, even when we were dead in trespasses, made us alive together with Christ (by grace you have been saved" (Ephesians 2:4-5 NKJV).

It is written: "By this we know love, because He laid down His life for us. And we also ought to lay down our lives for the brethren" (1 John 3:16 NKJV).

John, the apostle, wrote the following, ""In this is love, not that we loved God, but that He loved us and sent His Son to be the propitiation for our sins" (1 John 4:10 NKJV).

Romans 5:8 declares: "God demonstrated His own love toward us, in that while we were still sinners, Christ died for us" (Romans 5:8 NKJV).

Paul, the apostle, wrote the following in the letter to the Romans: "Now hope does not disappoint, because the love of God has been poured out in our hearts by the Holy Spirit who was given to us" (Romans 5:5 NKJV).

The love of God has been revealed in the life, death, resurrection, ascension and intercession of Jesus Christ at God's right hand of omnipotent power. And God continues to pour out His love into the hearts of believers through the indwelling of the Holy Spirit throughout the centuries until today.

This is the love of God that has been hidden throughout the ages but has NOW been revealed to us in Christ Jesus. No greater love has there ever been in the world, is there in the world at this moment, and no greater love will there ever be.

This love dominated the life of Paul the apostle while he lived on earth. He said that the love of God constrained him or compelled him to preach the gospel to the people who did not know God (Read 2 Corinthians 5:14). Paul the apostle knew that God had saved him from his sins and that it was the love of God which gave Jesus Christ to this world. This same love was working in Paul (Read John 17:26) and compelled him to preach the gospel. This same love of God should also be the driving force that moves us to share the only gospel that can save people from their sins. When we are filled with the love of God we are filled with the fullness of God and we will be able to lay down our lives for those God called us to serve.

Paul prayed the following for the church in Ephesus:

> "I pray that… Christ may dwell in your hearts through faith— that you, being rooted and grounded in love, may have strength to comprehend with all the saints what is the breadth and length and height and depth, and to know the love of Christ that surpasses knowledge, that you may be filled with all the fullness of God." (Ephesians 3:17-19 ESV)

Only if we are born again by the Spirit of God can we be filled with the Spirit of God and the love God. God gave Jesus Christ to this world so that those who would believe may be filled with His love so that they may also lay down their lives for the world in order that many may become the children of God. God has a general love for all the people of the world but a specific love for his elect.

# 2

## THE FOUNDATIONS OF EVANGELISM (PART 2; THE INSTRUMENTS IN THE WORK OF EVANGELISM)

### 2.9 KNOWING GOD SAVINGLY AND PERSONALLY

When we look at the people God has used in the Old and New Testament we see they were people who knew God personally and were called by God for the work of making God known. In the Old Testament Moses was called to lead the people out of Egypt and he later wrote the first five books of the Bible. Later, we see David, a man called by God who was anointed to be king of Israel and who wrote many of the Psalms which contained the gospel. And so we can go on through the Old Testament. The prophets Jeremiah and Isaiah were called by God to be prophets unto God (Read Jeremiah 1:1-10; Isaiah 6:1-8). They were called to bring the Word of God to the people of God. They preached the Word of God, using the law to bring conviction of sin, but they also preached the gospel, giving promises and hope for those who repent.

In the New Testament we see a similar pattern of people being called by God and commissioned to be his spokespersons. John the Baptist was set aside from the womb to be a prophet of God who would proclaim the Word of God. The twelve apostles were called by God to learn from Jesus and then sent out to preach the gospel of the kingdom to every village in Israel. And so God called Paul to be an apostle to share the Word of God and to preach the gospel. The apostles knew Jesus intimately because they lived and talked with Him for about three years. Paul says that he counted everything as rubbish in comparison to knowing Jesus Christ as his Lord and Saviour (Read Philippians 3:7-9). The greatest thing for Paul was not to preach the gospel but to know Jesus Christ intimately.

> "But whatever gain I had, I counted as loss for the sake of Christ. Indeed, I count everything as loss because of the surpassing worth of knowing Christ Jesus my Lord. For his sake I have suffered the loss of all things and count them as rubbish, in order that I may gain Christ." (Philippians 3:7-8 ESV)

When Jesus started His ministry he said the following:

> ""Not everyone who says to me, 'Lord, Lord,' will enter the kingdom of heaven, but the one who does the will of my Father who is in heaven. On that day many will say to me, 'Lord, Lord, did we not prophesy in your name, and cast out demons in your name, and do many mighty works in your name?' And then I will declare to them, 'I never knew you; depart from me, you workers of lawlessness.'" (Matthew 7:21-23 ESV)

To know God and to be known by God is more important than sharing the gospel. In heaven one day the work of evangelism to save the lost will be over. There will be no more need to evangelize and share the gospel to win the lost. What is of utmost importance is not preaching the Word of God, but knowing Jesus Christ savingly and personally. If a person is not genuinely converted he shouldn't be involved in the work of evangelism.

John the apostle made this point also very clear in his gospel.

> "And this is eternal life, that they know you the only true God, and Jesus Christ whom you have sent." (John 17:3 ESV)

47

And the apostle Peter emphasized this point of increasing in the experiential knowledge of Jesus Christ!

> "For if these qualities (faith, virtue, knowledge, self control, steadfastness, godliness, brotherly love, love) are yours and are increasing, they keep you from being ineffective or unfruitful in the knowledge of our Lord Jesus Christ." (2 Peter 1:8 ESV)

> "But grow in the grace and knowledge of our Lord and Savior Jesus Christ. To him be the glory both now and to the day of eternity. Amen."(2 Peter 3:18 ESV)

The gospels and the New Testament make it very clear that knowing Jesus Christ for who He is is essential in a person's life. It is the goal of the gospel. We preach the gospel not only because people are in danger of eternal hell and under the wrath of God, but because people are not reconciled to God and cut off from the true knowledge of God. We preach the gospel because people don't know God savingly and intimately. When we have that personal sweet relationship with God through Jesus Christ and the Holy Spirit the love of God compels us to make Him known so that others may enjoy that sweet communion with God as well. We want other people to know the blessedness and joy of knowing that their sins are forgiven as well.

Knowing God savingly and personally should be the driving force of doing great exploits for God. God drew us into the fellowship of the Trinity (Read John 6:44) and so now that we are satisfied in Him we want other people to be satisfied with His presence as well. Jesus said: "I am the bread of life. He who comes to Me shall never hunger, and he who believes in Me shall never thirst" (John 6:35 NKJV). We are called by God not ultimately to preach the Word and call others to repentance but to know God and make Him known. This is the foundation of our evangelizing. Knowing God is not a means to do something greater. Knowing God is the foundation of and the glorious end of our existence. God made us so that we might have eternal fellowship with Him. Evangelizing people, working for God, shouldn't be a greater thing than spending time alone with God and enjoying His presence! Having sweet fellowship with God, knowing Him better, should be the controlling force and blazing centre of one's existence. Without knowing God as one's personal Saviour and Lord no one should attempt to evangelize and preach the gospel.

> "Satisfy us in the morning with your steadfast love, that we may rejoice and be glad all our days." (Psalms 90:14 ESV)

## 2.10 THE BAPTISM, POWER AND ANOINTING OF THE HOLY SPIRIT

Some people think that the baptism of the Holy Spirit must include speaking in unknown languages. They appeal to the book of Acts chapter two when the Holy Spirit was poured out as a powerful reality upon the church. We do believe that we live now, since Pentecost, in the administration of the Spirit, where the Holy Spirit lives in His fullness, in every true believer of God. In Old Testament times the Holy Spirit did indwell believers, but not all were in-dwelt in the same way as now, or equipped for the work of ministry. While He was on earth Jesus Himself promised to send the Holy Spirit after He went to heaven. Before Christ was incarnated, crucified and ascended into heaven about 2000 years ago, the Holy Spirit was not an abiding, powerful reality in every believer's life although believers in the Old Testament were saved through faith in the promised Messiah and did experience the work and indwelling of the Holy Spirit to some degree (Read Psalm 51:11). But since Jesus went to heaven we live now in the administration of the abiding fullness of the Holy Spirit. Jesus said:

> "On the last day of the feast, the great day, Jesus stood up and cried out, "If anyone thirsts, let him come to me and drink. Whoever believes in me, as the Scripture has said, 'Out of his heart will flow rivers of living water.'" Now this he said about the Spirit, whom those who believed in him were to receive, for as yet the Spirit had not been given, because Jesus was not yet glorified." (John 7:37-39 ESV)

Every believer in Christ in the Old and New Testaments and today has been and is born again by the Spirit of God. Although the Holy Spirit gave the first disciples coherent languages at Pentecost we must not think the baptism of the Holy Spirit always includes the speaking of foreign languages. When a person believes in Jesus Christ unto salvation it shows that he/she is born again (Read 1 John 5:1; John 1:12,13). Being regenerated by the Holy Spirit and receiving the baptism of the Holy Spirit are not the same experience. Being born of the Spirit is the initial experience when a person becomes alive spiritually and experiences the heinousness of his sins and realizes he stands condemned and guilty before God. He experiences the pains of spiritual birth and starts crying out for forgiveness and salvation. The seed of regeneration is implanted in a person by God, but it is only after a person repents of his sins, acknowledges his own sins, and believes in Christ that he receives the gift of the Holy Spirit or is baptized by the Spirit (Galatians 3:14). Every believer in Christ has been baptized in the Holy Spirit. Paul makes this very clear in his first letter to the Corinthians.

> "For just as the body is one and has many members, and all the members of the body, though many, are one body, so it is with Christ. For in one Spirit we were all baptized into one body— Jews or Greeks, slaves or free—and all were made to drink of one Spirit." (Corinthians 12:12-13 ESV)

Some Christian groups in the world want to make us believe that if you don't speak in unknown languages you haven't been baptized by the Holy Spirit. This teaching is not according to sound doctrine. Paul says here that all Christians were made to drink of the same Spirit, meaning being baptized in the Holy Spirit. We are commanded by the Scriptures to be filled with the Holy Spirit (Read Ephesians 5:18) and to pray for the fullness of the Holy Spirit (See Ephesians 3:15-20). Christians can walk in the power of the Spirit. Jesus promised the disciples before Pentecost that they will receive power when the Holy Spirit comes upon them and that they would be witnesses of Christ (See Acts 1:8). This promise of receiving the power of the Holy Spirit in Christ is true for all believers throughout all ages, since Pentecost. In fact, Paul prayed for the Ephesian Christians that:

> "... God.....may give to you the spirit of wisdom and revelation in the knowledge of Him, the eyes of your understanding being enlightened; that you may know what is the hope of His calling, what are the riches of the glory of His inheritance in the saints, and what is the exceeding greatness of His power toward us who believe, according to the working of His mighty power which He worked in Christ when He raised Him from the dead and

seated Him at His right hand in the heavenly places, far above all principality and power and might and dominion, and every name that is named, not only in this age but also in that which is to come" (Ephesians 1:17-21 NKJV).

It is written:

"For God has not given us a spirit of fear, but of power and of love and of a sound mind." (II Timothy 1:7 NKJV)

Because the Holy Spirit can be quenched (Read 1 Thessalonians 5:19) and grieved (See Ephesians 4:30) when we as believers sin, we ought to confess (See 1 John 1:9) and repent (Read Proverbs 28:13) of our sins regularly in order to walk in the power of the Holy Spirit. God's will for the believer is that we always walk in step with the Spirit and not according to the flesh and sinful desires. God's will is that the believer mortify the deeds of the body on a daily basis (Read Romans 8:13, Matthew 16:24,25).

When a person is born again and baptized by the Spirit of God he receives the anointing of the Holy Spirit (Read 1 John 2:20). All believers in Christ are anointed by the Holy Spirit and all must be filled continually with the Holy Spirit (Read Ephesians 5:18). In the Old Testament the kings, priests and prophets were anointed for specific tasks they had to administer. They were equipped by the Spirit of God for their offices, although many were rebellious and didn't worship the true God, especially the kings. In the New Testament we see that all believers are called to be prophets, priests and kings (Read Revelation 1:5; 1 Peter 2:9). In other words, all believers are anointed to represent God on earth as His kings, to rule over sin, Satan and the corruption of the world. We are anointed to be priests representing Christ by praying for the church and the lost and the unreached and we are commissioned to share and preach and proclaim the gospel as prophets (Read Ephesians 6:15; 1 Peter 2:9 Mark 16:15). All Christians are called to proclaim the gospel and to be God's witnesses because we have received the Spirit of Christ, and the testimony of Christ.

The anointing we as believers were given, means God has equipped us with His Spirit to speak forth His Word. This anointing was not given to all believers in the Old Testament. Old Testament believers were not all equipped for the work of the ministry.

> "So everyone who acknowledges me before men, I also will acknowledge before my Father who is in heaven, but whoever denies me before men, I also will deny before my Father who is in heaven" (Matthew 10:32-33 ESV).

Paul the apostle said:

> "I am not ashamed of the gospel for it is the power of God for salvation to everyone who believes..." (Romans 1:16,17 ESV).

The presence, power, anointing and baptism of the Holy Spirit equip the believer to be an evangelist: to be successful and to convict the world of sin, righteousness and judgement (Read John 16:8). When we obey God in evangelism and witnessing, the Holy Spirit will do the work of convicting sinners. The power is in the Word (See 1 Peter 1:23-25) and the gospel of God, not in us. We are mere jars of clay that easily break. The power is in God (See 2 Cor 4:1-4). Without the Spirit's baptism, power and anointing all our efforts in evangelizing believers and unbelievers will be useless and futile. We have to be regenerated by the Holy Spirit first of all, and then led, equipped and moved by Him in this great work set before us.

## 2.11 THE NEED FOR PURITY AND HOLINESS IN THE EVANGELIST'S LIFE

In this day and age it is essential for any Christian, but especially the Christian worker and evangelist to be holy and keep himself pure. We hear of so many pastors and leaders who fall into sexual sin that ruins their ministries. King David, Samson and Solomon are examples of men who were strong and wise, but who succumbed to temptation. If these men in the Bible fell into grievous sin, we must not think we are not susceptible to the same dangers! "Therefore let him who thinks he stands take heed lest he fall" (1 Corinthians 10:12 NKJV).

In order to know God more intimately and be filled with the Holy Spirit continually and see God's glory, we must remain pure. Jesus said: "Blessed are the pure in heart for they shall see God" (Matthew 5:8 ESV). Although God can and does use people who are clean or unclean to fulfil his purposes, if we want God to use us for honourable purposes we have to cleanse ourselves from what is dishonourable. If we do so we will be useful to God and be ready for every good work! God does His greatest works through those who live holy and pure lives!

> "Now in a great house there are not only vessels of gold and silver but also of wood and clay, some for honorable use, some for dishonorable. Therefore, if anyone cleanses himself from what is dishonorable, he will be a vessel for honorable use, set apart as holy, useful to the master of the house, ready for every good work. So flee youthful passions and pursue righteousness, faith, love, and peace, along with those who call on the Lord from a pure heart." (2 Timothy 2:20-22 ESV)

We should ask: How do we cleanse ourselves? What does this cleansing involve? What must I do to cleanse myself thoroughly so that I can be a vessel for noble and honourable use? The Bible tells us the way to be cleansed: Firstly, we are cleansed by the blood of Jesus!

> "But if we walk in the light as He is in the light, we have fellowship with one another, and the blood of Jesus Christ His Son cleanses us from all sin" (1 John 1:7 NKJV).

No cleansing can take place unless the blood of Jesus washes us. But take note when it is that the blood of Jesus becomes effective: it is when we walk in the light as God is in the light. This statement begs the question: what does it mean to walk in the light as God is in the light? The answer is found later in the same passage:

> "If we say we have no sin, we deceive ourselves, and the truth is not in us. If we confess our sins, he is faithful and just to forgive us our sins and to cleanse us from all unrighteousness. If we say we have not sinned, we make him a liar, and his word is not in us" (1 John 1:8-10 ESV).

We are thoroughly cleansed from our sins when we confess our sins to God, our sins in the past (verse 10) and all the sins that we are aware of at present (verse 8). If we hide our sins from God and keep something in the dark we will not receive proper cleansing. James 5:16 commands "...confess your sins to one another and pray for one another, that you may we be healed" (James 5:16). The best way to do a thorough job of confessing is to take an inventory of your life regularly and ask the Holy Spirit to remind you of anything in your life, past and present, that causes Him grief. If you do this God will bring sins to your mind that you can confess. Confessing of one's sins means basically to agree with God about the things that are sinful and wrong in your life. In order to walk in truth with God it is essential to humble ourselves before God and confess our sins to Him. In the case of sins that we struggle with it is advisable to have an accountability partner, some mature Christian or pastor, and to confess your sins to another. I know in my life how God has helped me to overcome sins as I brought sins into the light before a brother. This is not a legalistic rule that always must be followed but a help in a believer's life if you find yourself in a rut and unable to overcome your defilement.

But confession of sins is not enough. We must forsake our sins, and thorough repentance is necessary.

> "He who covers his sins will not prosper, But whoever confesses and forsakes them will have mercy" (Proverbs 28:13 NKJV).

We have to repent Biblically in order to be an instrument of honourable use to our Master. Biblical repentance involves: conviction, contrition and conversion. God has to convict us of our sins. A change of mind must take place. Then we must have a broken and contrite heart over our sins. God must show us and we must feel how we have offended Him by our sins. We must have godly sorrow over our sins, not only in the beginning of our Christian walk but throughout our Christian walk (Read James 4:8-10; 2 Corinthians 7:10). God must work in such a way that you loathe your sins and hate your sins against God. We must come to realize that our sins caused the crucifixion of Christ. Our sins nailed Jesus to the cross. Our sins were responsible for His death.

> "Draw near to God, and he will draw near to you. Cleanse your hands, you sinners, and purify your hearts, you double-minded. Be wretched and mourn and weep. Let your laughter be turned to mourning and your joy to gloom. Humble yourselves before the Lord, and he will exalt you." (James 4:8-10 ESV)

And then Biblical repentance also involves conversion, a change of behaviour. Unless we continually turn from our sins we haven't really repented. God doesn't only want to change our thinking (See Romans 12:1,2) and feelings (Read Psalm 37:4), but our behaviour. God wants us to live in ways that bring Him glory.

To be holy and clean are necessary to be effective for every good work in God's kingdom. How will a surgeon in a hospital, who is about to do an operation, be effective if his instruments are defiled and dirty? He will cause great damage to the patient he is operating on. He wouldn't dare to use dirty and defiled knives and instruments. So God wants to use clean and holy instruments to build his kingdom and church. If we are thoroughly cleansed we will be useful for every good work in God's hands!

Back to our question: How then shall we be thoroughly cleansed? We said firstly by the blood (atonement) of Jesus Christ. But everyone is not automatically cleansed by the blood of Jesus. It is by faith that we are cleansed (Read Acts 15:9). Our hearts are cleansed as we confess our sins in truth, as we turn away from our sins (Biblical repentance) and as we believe that Jesus died and paid the highest price for our forgiveness and cleansing! But that is not all! It is believing the Word of God and in the promises of God that cleanses us! Jesus said:

> "Already you are clean because of the word that I have spoken to you." (John 15:3 ESV)

And:

> "Husbands, love your wives, as Christ loved the church and gave himself up for her, that he might sanctify her, having cleansed her by the washing of water with the word, so that he might present the church to himself in splendor, without spot or wrinkle or any such thing, that she might be holy and without blemish." (Ephesians 5:25-27 ESV)

And the psalmist teaches us:

> "How can a young man keep his way pure? By guarding it according to your word" (Psalm 119:9 ESV)

> I have stored up your word in my heart, that I might not sin against you." (Psalms 119:11 ESV)

We are cleansed and purified as we meditate on the Word of God day and night (See Psalm 1:1-4), as we drink in the Word of God, as we read it and internalize it and delight in it and apply it to our lives. The Word of God washes us and directs us and shows us the character of God. The Word helps us to gaze upon the beauty and glory of Christ who transforms us from one degree of glory to another (Read 2 Corinthians 3:18). As we meditate on the Word of God day and night and delight in it, and make it our own, God will make us bear fruit in our season (See Psalm 1:1-4) and we will grow and be cleansed from our sins as we accompany the Word with repentance and faith in Christ.

Let us therefore make use of this means of grace: read, study and meditate on the Word of God and apply the Word of God to your life! We will be blessed and purified not only if we are hearers of the Word but doers as Jesus taught us! Let us therefore listen to the Word of God as it is preached, in order to be honourable instruments in the Master's hand!

## 2.12 PRIVATE AND CORPORATE PRAYER

It is very clear in the gospel that we must know that the power of the conversion of sinners is not in us, but in God. Our sufficiency is not in ourselves but in God and from God. "Blessed are the meek for they shall inherit the earth" (Matthew 5:5 ESV). "Blessed are the poor in spirit for theirs is the kingdom of God" (Matthew 5:3 ESV). Prayer is the channel whereby we access the infinite resources and strength and salvation of God. We come to God and know we are bankrupt spiritually in and of ourselves but we bank on the infinite power of God to make us willing and able to do His will and display the nature of Christ.

Prayer is the power of evangelism. It is the means God has ordained by which He will save the lost and build His church through the ministry of the Word. Jesus set the example for us, as did many other saints in the Bible (David, Moses, Paul, Ezra and Daniel), of humility before God. If Jesus Christ needed the early morning hours of the day to commune with God, how much more will we, who are sinful and so prone to temptation and sin? For us to know the will and mind of God and His strength as we minister His Word we need to spend a lot of time with Him alone. "Early will I seek You" (Psalm 63:1 NKJV), the psalmist prayed. Moses prayed: "Oh, satisfy us early with Your mercy, that we may rejoice and be glad all our days" (Psalm 90:14 NKJV). An evangelist who neglects his time alone with God (where he can commune with the Almighty) will soon succumb to sin and temptation and become ineffective in ministry. How can we withstand the fiery darts of the evil one if we are not praying people?

How much time do you spend in the Word of God daily, in prayer and drawing strength from God? Here is a suggestion: Make an appointment with God every day where you will spend time alone with Him. Put your cell phone away and your tablet and computer and get away from things that will distract you, and get alone with God! Turn off the radio and television and hear from God! Listen to the authoritative, complete and sufficient revelation of God in Holy Scripture. Let your words be few when you pray. God is not impressed by a lot of words. In fact He commanded us not to use vain repetitions like the heathen do when we pray. God knows what we need before we pray (See Matthew 6:6-8).

> "Likewise the Spirit helps us in our weakness. For we do not know what to pray for as we ought, but the Spirit himself intercedes for us with groanings too deep for words. And he who searches hearts knows what is the mind of the Spirit, because the Spirit intercedes for the saints according to the will of God" (Romans 8:26-27 ESV).

We don't know what to pray as we ought! If we are left to ourselves we will only pray for our own needs and wants. Our prayers will be self-centred and self-serving. Therefore, let the Word of God guide you in prayer. Let the agenda of God be your agenda. Let God's priorities be your priorities! Let the mind of God be your mind. You may ask: How do I pray according to the Spirit and the mind of God? The answer is simple! Let the Word of God guide you! In the Bible we find the mind of Christ. Jesus Christ set us the example when He taught us how to pray in Matthew 6:9-11. He showed us the parameters of our prayer-life.

> "Pray then like this:
> "Our Father in heaven,
> hallowed be your name.
> Your kingdom come,
> your will be done, on earth as it is in heaven.
> Give us this day our daily bread,
> and forgive us our debts,
> as we also have forgiven our debtors.
> And lead us not into temptation,
> but deliver us from evil." (Matthew 6:9-13 ESV)

If we look closely at this prayer we see the following:

God's glory, the coming of God's kingdom and the establishment of God's will in all things on earth as it is in heaven should be our focus in prayer. Our needs, our forgiveness, our protection and our guidance should be of secondary importance. They are not unimportant, but they are of secondary importance. That God's Name be hallowed and glorified; that God's kingdom should come in politics, in our schools, in our courts, in our families, in our businesses and everywhere on earth; that God's moral laws be obeyed and honoured; that all may hear the good news of the gospel (Read Mark 16:15); that disciples be made of all ethnic groups on the face of the earth (See Matthew 28:18-20); that labourers be sent out into God's harvest fields (Read Matthew 9:35-38), *et cetera*, should dominate our prayers.

This simple acrostic should also guide you in prayer: ACTS

A – Adoration – Adoring and worshipping and praising God for His greatness and love and grace and justice and all His divine perfections, should be present everyday while we pray. We see this principal so many times in the book of Psalms.

C – Confession – Ask God to make you aware of your sins and confess them with contrition towards God. Humble yourself before God and He will lift you up. "If we say we have no sin, we deceive ourselves, and the truth is not in us. If we confess our sins, he is faithful and just to forgive us our sins and to cleanse us from all unrighteousness" (1 John 1:8,9 ESV).

T – Thanksgiving – Thank God regularly (Read 1 Thessalonians 5:16) for the forgiveness of sins by the blood of Jesus. Thank Him in all things because that is the will of God. Know that everything we have and are has been given to us by God: resources, money, opportunities, daily necessities, salvation, the Holy Spirit, difficulties, and sufferings. Count your blessings one by one. What I sometimes do is to name 10 things to be thankful for in a day.

S – Supplication – Focus on God's priorities first (as noted above) but then pray also for your own needs and challenges and for those in your church, as well as for friends and family who are facing challenges.

Private prayer should include these things but especially in the work of evangelism we should also pray corporately together as a church and with Christian Ministries and Christians who know us well. I have been in many different churches and it has always been a great blessing to spend hours with other believers praying for the particular outreach or ministry or people in my fellowship. To pray corporately with other believers is not only an example in the Bible given to us to follow, but it is commanded in the Bible:

> "First of all, then, I urge that supplications, prayers, intercessions, and thanksgivings be made for all people, for kings and all who are in high positions, that we may lead a peaceful and quiet life, godly and dignified in every way" (1 Timothy 2:1-2 ESV).

> "I desire then that in every place the men should pray, lifting holy hands without anger or quarreling" (1 Timothy 2:8 ESV).

> "And they (the believers) devoted themselves to the apostles' teaching and the fellowship, to the breaking of bread and the prayers." (Acts 2:42 ESV)

> "Rejoice in hope, be patient in tribulation, be constant in prayer." (Romans 12:12 ESV)

> "Therefore, confess your sins to one another and pray for one another, that you may be healed. The prayer of a righteous person has great power as it is working." (James 5:16 ESV)

"praying at all times in the Spirit, with all prayer and supplication. To that end keep alert with all perseverance, making supplication for all the saints, and also for me, that words may be given to me in opening my mouth boldly to proclaim the mystery of the gospel, for which I am an ambassador in chains, that I may declare it boldly, as I ought to speak." (Ephesians 6:18-20 ESV)

The great apostle Paul asked that the church pray for him that he might proclaim the mystery of the gospel. He knew that in his own ability and wisdom and strength, it would not have been possible for the kingdom of God to go forward. As stated above, without a vibrant prayer life, privately and corporately, our efforts in making God known would be futile. Therefore, any person who endeavours to obey the Word of God by proclaiming and distributing and sharing the Word and gospel of God should be on their knees frequently, in private and with the local church and the ministry one is involved in. God has chosen to work through His church and to separate one's life from the prayer meeting at one's church or mission is to outrightly disobey God. Our evangelism and ministries for the Lord should be bathed in prayer and be bathed in the prayers of our fellow brothers and sisters in Christ. The work of evangelism and preaching the Word should never be divorced from private and corporate prayer. No soldier of God can withstand the onslaughts of the evil one without regular times of prayer and having a prayerful disposition! It is sheer lunacy and a sign of a proud heart to attempt to make God known without a prayer-life.

> "Rejoice always, pray without ceasing, give thanks in all circumstances; for this is the will of God in Christ Jesus for you." (1 Thessalonians 5:16-18 ESV)

May God grant us the focus, the desire, and the vision to be people of prayer. God will work as we bow down before Him in repentance and as we seek the coming of His kingdom and the glorification of His Name in all things!

# THE TEN COMMANDMENTS

**Introduction/Purposes of the law**

**The Ten Commandments**
1. The first Commandment: You shall have no other gods before Me
2. The Second Commandment: You shall not make for yourself an idol in the form of anything… You shall not bow down and worship them.
3. The Third Commandment: You shall not take the Name of the Lord in vain
4. The fourth Commandment: You shall keep the Sabbath holy
5. The firth Commandment: Honour your father and mother
6. The Sixth Commandment: You shall not murder
7. The Seventh Commandment: You shall not commit adultery
8. The Eight Commandment: You shall not steal
9. The Ninth Commandment: You shall not bear false testimony against your neighbour
10. The Tenth Commandment: You shall not covet

**Conclusion**

**Appendix II: Who is Jesus Christ really?**
**Appendix V: The marvellous love of God**
**Appendix IV: It is finished**
**Appendix VI: The glories of God's righteousness**
**Appendix III: Two Gates, Two Roads, Two Destinies**
**Appendix VI: Is Jesus Christ the only way to heaven?**

# INTRODUCTION/ PURPOSES
# OF THE LAW

The Ten Commandments given by God to Moses on Mount Sinai about 3500 years ago have eternal significance for the people of God and for the human race, and this for several reasons. We must remember that the Ten Commandments were never given to the people of God as a means to obtain or merit their salvation. We know this fact if we read the book of Exodus in its context. God initiated His plan to rescue the Israelites who were suffering under Pharaoh and the Egyptian people when He appeared to Moses in Arabia in a burning bush (See Exodus 3,4). By His outstretched arm and mighty miracles, God delivered His people from the most powerful country in the world at the time. God used Moses and Aaron as His instruments to deliver them from the oppression of false religion. God initiated the process and He executed His miracles by the hand of Moses. By the ten plagues God destroyed the livestock, resources, army, vegetation and firstborn of Egypt. He did this to show the world that there was no other God like Him. God made a Name for Himself by delivering the descendants of Abraham, Isaac and Jacob from the Egyptians. He remembered the covenant that He made with Abraham, Isaac and Jacob when He said that He would give them the land of Canaan as a lasting possession and that He would bless Abraham's descendants to be as many as the stars in the sky and the sand on the seashore (Read Genesis 15:5; 22:16,17). God kept His promise and His covenant of grace, as He is God who cannot lie (Read Numbers 23:19).

After He had delivered the Israelites from the Egyptian army and miraculously divided the Red Sea so that more than a million people went through the sea dry-shod, God led them through the desert. Then they camped at Mount Sinai, where God appeared to Moses in the burning bush. God fulfilled His promise yet again just as He told Moses He would (Read Exodus 3:7-12). He then told Moses to come up the mountain. For 40 days and 40 nights Moses was on top of Mount Sinai and God gave him these commandments engraved with His own finger on two tablets of stone. While this was happening, God came down in a cloud and the people witnessed thundering, lightning flashes, the sound of the trumpet and the mountain smoking. He came down upon the mountain but His appearance was veiled from the people.

The law of God was given **after** He delivered the descendants of Abraham from Egypt, not before. The last of the ten Plagues was called the 'death of the firstborn' and before the angel of death killed all the firstborn in Egypt, God instituted the Passover. God commanded the Israelites to slaughter lambs and put the blood of the lambs on the doorposts that night. Because the blood was put on the doorposts and because the Passover lambs died, He overlooked and covered the sins of His people and no firstborn Israelite died in Egypt that night. The Passover lambs in Egypt and throughout subsequent generations in Israel pointed to the work of redemption that God prepared through His only begotten Son Jesus Christ, Who would redeem His people from their sins by offering Himself centuries later. Jesus Christ is called the Passover Lamb and the Lamb who was slain, who takes away the sin of the world (Read John 1:29; 1 Corinthians 5:7). So, the law of God was never given as a means to free us from the slavery of sin, the world and the devil, but it was given so that we can know the will of God and live in a way He wants us to live. The covenant that He instituted at Sinai was a covenant of grace, but as in every covenant that God instituted there were covenant obligations or 'terms and conditions' that His people should keep; not as a means to obtain salvation but as a rule of life and to keep good relationship with the God of the Universe. So, the law of God given by Moses, the Decalogue (or Ten Commandments) were given as a rule of life.

The Decalogue also has other functions and purposes. Firstly, the Ten Commandments show us and reveal to us the nature and character of God. They show us what kind of a God He is and what He is like (God cannot give something more honour than Himself, He cannot commit idolatry). God exists to glorify Himself and to enjoy Himself forever (John Piper: The Pleasures of God). If He didn't, He would be committing idolatry. The Bible tells us that God is holy and righteous and just. God cannot lie (See Numbers 23:19). He cannot steal, be greedy, dishonour His own Name, and so on. When we look at the Ten Commandments we see God's holiness and His Justice. We see that God will by no means clear the guilty (Read Exodus 20:5; 34:6,7) and that He will punish those who dishonour Him. "The law is holy, and the commandment is holy and just and good" (Romans 7:12 NKJV), as God Himself is.

Secondly, the law shows us the nature of sin and that it is exceedingly sinful (Read Romans 7:13). The Ten Commandments give us, "the knowledge of sin" (Romans 3:20 NKJV) and it shows us that we all stand guilty before God (See Romans 3:19) and are therefore worthy to be punished (Read Romans 3:23; 6:23; Genesis 2:17). The Ten Commandments show us that we are helpless, carnal and "sold under sin" (Romans 7:14 NKJV). The law is our schoolmaster and our tutor to show us that God is holy and we are sinful and that we desperately need a Saviour (Read Galatians 3:24). The law leads and guides us to Christ, who can justify us by His blood and righteousness.

And lastly, the law of God and the Ten Commandments have been given by God to restrain evil. We can say that, the law revives sin, as Paul said (Read Romans 7:8,9): before we knew the law we didn't know what sin was. But if the government in any country punishes the evildoers and rewards the righteous as they should, then it instils fear in the citizens of that country. We know of no country that is applying the punishments of law of God consistently, but we do see that every country enforces aspects of the Ten Commandments to a degree and therefore it has a measure of restraining evil in society. Even in many societies, some of them barbaric and primitive through the ages, people have the law of God written on their hearts, just as the book of Romans tell us (See Romans 2:12-16).

Each of the *Ten Commandments* deals with a family of sins. We must understand the Ten Commandments in the light of the figure of speech called "synecdoche." Synecdoche is a literary device in which a part of something represents the whole or it may be used that the whole represents a part of something. In the case of the Ten Commandments, the part, (e.g. 'You shall have no other gods before Me' represents the whole (satanism, animism, pantheism, necrolatry, atheism etc.). Each commandment also calls us to specific God-honouring actions, attitudes and dispositions. The fact that the Ten Commandments are stated negatively (e.g. You shall not murder) doesn't mean that the positive command "love your neighbour" and "value human life" isn't implied. And here, the figure of speech, synecdoche, should be applied. Each commandment calls us to many God honouring actions, attitudes and dispositions of character.

My prayer is that as you go through these commandments and as you go through these lessons you will see God in a new light, that you will see that they speak to your conscience, convicting you of sin and God's righteousness, and that they draw you to Christ Jesus for forgiveness. I pray that you see them not only as things that you shouldn't do but as speaking to you and showing you what God wants you to do and say and think and feel, in every area of your life.

Nico van Zyl
www.interethnicmissions.net

# THE TEN COMMANDMENTS:

"And God spoke all these words, saying:

"I am the LORD your God, who brought you out of the land of Egypt, out of the house of bondage.

"You shall have no other gods before Me.

"You shall not make for yourself a carved image—any likeness of anything that is in heaven above, or that is in the earth beneath, or that is in the water under the earth; you shall not bow down to them nor serve them. For I, the LORD your God, am a jealous God, visiting the iniquity of the fathers upon the children to the third and fourth generations of those who hate Me, but showing mercy to thousands, to those who love Me and keep My commandments.

"You shall not take the name of the LORD your God in vain, for the LORD will not hold him guiltless who takes His name in vain.

"Remember the Sabbath day, to keep it holy. Six days you shall labor and do all your work, but the seventh day is the Sabbath of the LORD your God. In it you shall do no work: you, nor your son, nor your daughter, nor your male servant, nor your female servant, nor your cattle, nor your stranger who is within your gates. For in six days the LORD made the heavens and the earth, the sea, and all that is in them, and rested the seventh day. Therefore, the LORD blessed the Sabbath day and hallowed it.

"Honor your father and your mother, that your days may be long upon the land which the LORD your God is giving you.

"You shall not murder.

"You shall not commit adultery.

"You shall not steal.

"You shall not bear false witness against your neighbor.

"You shall not covet your neighbor's house; you shall not covet your neighbor's wife, nor his male servant, nor his female servant, nor his ox, nor his donkey, nor anything that is your neighbor's."

**Now all the people witnessed the thunderings, the lightning flashes, the sound of the trumpet, and the mountain smoking; and when the people saw it, they trembled and stood afar off. Then they said to Moses, "You speak with us, and we will hear; but let not God speak with us, lest we die." And Moses said to the people, "Do not fear; for God has come to test you, and that His fear may be before you, so that you may not sin." So the people stood afar off, but Moses drew near the thick darkness where God was." (Exodus 20:1-21 NKJV)**

The first four Commandments deal with our relationship with God.

The last six Commandments deal with our relationship with our neighbours and fellow human beings.

### Deuteronomy 6:4-7

"Hear O Israel: The Lord our God, the Lord is One. You shall love the Lord your God with all your heart and with all your soul and with all your strength. And these words which I command you today shall be in your heart. You shall teach them diligently to your children, and shall talk of them when you sit in your house, when you walk by the way, when you lie down, and when you rise up" (Deuteronomy 6:4-7 NKJV).

### Ecclesiastes 12:13

"Let us hear the conclusion of the whole matter: Fear God and keep his commandments, for this is man's all" (Ecclesiastes 12:13 NKJV).

Jesus summed up the Ten Commandments and the Law by saying:

### Matthew 22:37-40

Jesus said to him: "you shall love the Lord your God with all your heart, with all your sou, and with all your mind. This is the first and great commandment. And the second is like it: you shall love your neighbor as yourself. On these two commandments hang all the Law and the Prophets" (Matthew 22:37-40 NKJV).

## 1. "You shall have no other gods before Me" (Exodus 20:3)
## Area: God

The Bible reveals that there is only one God in the universe (Read Isaiah 46:10,11; Deuteronomy 6:4,5; 1 Kings 8:60) and that He alone should be worshipped. God commands us in the first commandment that we should always be satisfied with Him for who He is (Father, Son and Holy Spirit, eternally existent in three Persons), what He stands for and for how He revealed Himself in Scripture and in general revelation. Jesus said it so beautifully in Matthew 22:37: "You shall love the Lord your God with all your heart, with all your soul and all your mind" (Matthew 22:37 NKJV). Moses prayed to God, "satisfy us in the morning with your steadfast love that we may rejoice and be glad all our days" (Psalm 90:14 ESV). To be satisfied with all that God was, is, and will be for us in Christ Jesus through the presence and the power of the Holy Spirit, is what worshipping God is all about. God doesn't only require us to sing praises to Him, but that our whole lives be worship unto Him. That is the meaning of Romans 12:1, 2. When we give our bodies to God, continually, as living sacrifices, we worship Him.

David prayed this after He received revelation from God, "How precious is your lovingkindness, O God, therefore the children of men put their trust under the shadow of Your wings. They are abundantly satisfied with the fullness of Your house; and You give them drink from the river of Your pleasures" (Psalm 36:7-9 NKJV). Jesus Christ is portrayed as the Fountain of life and Living Waters in John 6:35; John 4:14 and John 7:37-39. When we come to Jesus and believe in Him as the Bible says, we are forgiven our sins and He fills us with the Holy Spirit. Therefore, Jesus promised in John 6:35: "...whoever comes to me shall not hunger, and whoever believes in me shall never thirst" John (6:35 ESV). As theologian John Piper said: "God is most glorified in us when we are most satisfied in Him." When we come to Jesus to satisfy our deepest desires we are filled by the Holy Spirit (Read Ephesians 3:15-18; 5:18) and the love of God. Only when we receive Christ Jesus for who He is can we worship and glorify Him aright. Only by the Holy Spirit in us can we worship and love and honour God as He should be, but even then, our worship falls short, because we are fallen, sinful human beings, even though we are born of the Holy Spirit (Read Romans 7:14-25).

**The Heidelberg Catechism** says the following of the first commandment: "That I, as sincerely as I desire the salvation of my own soul, avoid and flee from all idolatry, sorcery, soothsaying, superstition, invocation of saints, or any other creatures, and learn rightly to know the only true God, trust in Him alone, with all humility and patience submit to Him, expect all good things from Him only, love, fear and glorify Him with my whole heart, so that I renounce and forsake all creatures rather than commit even the least thing contrary to His will."

We see by this definition that God must rule supremely in our hearts to obey this command. He must have the supremacy in our souls, in our thinking, speaking, feeling and acting. This is the meaning of Matthew 13:44-46. Jesus **must** be the pearl of great price in one's heart and the treasure for which one is willing to forsake all else.

The following things are forbidden by this commandment:

**Polytheism**: the belief and the worship of more than one god. In Hinduism we find this. The ancient Greeks and Romans also worshipped many gods. Christians worship one God, although He is distinct in three personalities. God is one in essence, one in will and purpose, but separated in the roles they play in the universe.

**Pantheism:** the doctrine that God is in everything. We cannot worship God in birds or in animals or in nature in the sense that God is in the creatures He made. God is distinct from what He has made although God's divine attributes can be seen in nature, such as His power or judgement or compassion. God is omnipresent but distinct from what He has made. Isaiah 46:5 states: "To whom shall you liken Me, and make Me equal, and compare Me, that we may be alike?" (Isaiah 46:5 NKJV).

**Animism:** the belief that all living things have a living soul.

**Spiritism**: making contact with evil spirits or attempting to make contact with dead people and trusting in them.

**Shamanism**: Using a spiritist or witch doctor to make contact with the unseen world to prevent bad fortune and secure favour.

**Necrolatry**: the worship of people who have died. Animism, spiritism, shamanism and necrolatry usually go hand in hand in tribal and African cultures untouched by the gospel of Christ. These practices are clearly forbidden by God in Deuteronomy 18:10-12.

**Satanism/Occultism**: the worship of Satan also called Lucifer the fallen angel and fascination with the evil-supernatural world.

**Humanism**: making man and his thoughts the measure of all things. Humanism worships man, his abilities, his achievements, whether it be in scientific discovery, scientific or medical inventions, sport, political, artistic or academic achievements and revering and fearing and adoring mankind above and instead of God (See Romans 1:18-25). The chief sin in humanism is **pride**.

**Atheism**: the belief that there is no God. The Bible calls these people fools because what is evident about God can be clearly perceived in what He has made (See Psalm 14:1; Romans 1:18-22).

**Fortune-telling:** a person who claims to foretell future events

**Love of money:** Jesus said we cannot serve God and money at the same time. We will love the one and despise the other (See Matthew 6:24). The Bible calls, "the love of money a root of all kinds of evil" (1 Timothy 6:10 ESV). Money in itself is not wrong but to make an idol of it and centering one's life on money and not on God is idolatry.

---If anything in your life becomes more important to you than God, a wife, a husband, a child, children, your job, your career, sex within marriage, food, alcohol or any other legitimate thing, it becomes idolatry. God has given many things in our lives to enjoy, but if those things we enjoy, the gifts of God, become the centre of our affections then it is sin and idolatry. God must be the centre of our trust. Jesus Christ alone obtained and secured eternal peace and salvation for us who believe. Trusting in anyone or anything else is idolatry.

**Scripture to consider:** Jesus said: "Whoever loves father or mother more than me is not worthy of me: and whoever loves son or daughter more than me is not worthy of me. And whoever does not take his cross and follow me, is not worthy of me" (Matthew 10:37,38 ESV). Jesus must always have the pre-eminence (See Colossians 1:18) in our lives. Let every idol be dethroned in your life and let Him reign supreme!

> **2. "You shall not make for yourself a carved image – any likeness of anything that is in heaven above, or that is in the earth beneath, or that is in the water under the earth; you shall not bow down to them nor serve them" (Exodus 20:4-5 NKJV) Area: Worship**

One thing we should understand about God is that He is incomprehensible, yet knowable. He has revealed Himself so that we can understand His will and purposes for us. The Bible says, "The secret things belong to Lord our God, but those things which are revealed belong to us and to our children forever" (Deuteronomy 29:29 NKJV). God made space, time, energy and matter, but He is greater and outside everything He created, even though He is present everywhere (See Psalm 139:7-12). He inhabits eternity, "from everlasting to everlasting you are God" (Psalm 90:1 NKJV), yet He lives with the contrite and humble in heart (See Isaiah 57:13). God is far greater than human beings, yet He has made us in His image (Read Genesis 1:27,28) so that we can have a saving relationship with Him. God has made everything that exists, and He deserves all our worship. Because "God is Spirit" (John 4:24 NKJV) we must worship Him "in Spirit and truth" (John 4:24 NKJV). That is what Jesus Christ revealed to the Samaritan woman in Israel (John 4:23). God doesn't live in the Temple anymore, as He did in Old Testament times. He doesn't live between the Ark of the Covenant, as in the times when the Israelites travelled through the desert or when the Temple was built in Jerusalem.

We cannot make an image of God and think it resembles Him in any way, because He is far superior to, and greater and bigger than, anything He has created, be it animals on land, birds in the air or fish or anything He has made in the sea. To make an image of God would be to bring Him to our level. God, however, is infinite. His presence is unlimited and infinite, so is His understanding; His ways and thoughts are above our ways and thoughts (Read Isaiah 55:6,7). His ways cannot be traced (See Romans 11:33-36). The earth we live on is like a dust particle in God's eyes in comparison to how big the universe is, and God is bigger than the Universe! He made matter and space! Therefore, to make a carved image or any image of God is forbidden because we would misrepresent God and that would be a lie. It is written, "For now we see in a mirror, dimly, but then face to face. Now I know in part, but then I shall know just as I also am known" (1 Corinthians 13:12 NKJV).

Not only are we not to make an image of God, but we are also not permitted to bow down to an image of God or to serve and worship it. This was the sin of the Israelites when God delivered them from the bondage of the Egyptians. When Moses received the 10 commandments of God and stayed away for 40 days, the Israelites made a golden calf and worshipped it as if the *calf* was the one who delivered them from Egypt. The nations around the world in many cultures make images of what they believe to be God, like in India, where they literally make carved and molten images of their gods and bow down to them and worship them. The true God and Creator of the world on the other hand ought to be worshipped in Spirit and in truth by faith (See John 4:23,24; 2 Corinthians 5:7). We are commended by God if we come to Him in faith, believing His promises and trusting in His character and how He has revealed Himself in His Word (See Hebrews 11:1-6). The apostle Paul told us what true worship is: "…endeavoring to keep the unity of the Spirit in the bond of peace. There is one body and one Spirit, just as you were called in one hope of your calling; one Lord, one faith, one baptism; one God and Father of all, who is above all, and through all, and in you all" (Ephesians 4:3-6 NKJV).

The **Heidelberg Catechism** says the following about the second commandment: "That we in no wise represent God by images, nor worship Him in any other way than He has commanded in His word." Question 97 asks: Are images then not at all to be tolerated? Answer: "God may not be represented by any means. But as to creatures, though they may be represented, yet God forbids to make, or to have resemblance of them, either in order to worship them or to serve God by them." We must realize that the Roman Catholic "Church" made images of God in their art forms over the centuries and used them to resemble God, because the common people could not read the Bible for themselves because the printing press did not exist before the 15th century. The Reformers were against these practices because they were unbiblical.

God forbids the following things by the second commandment:

**Idolatry of statues:** statues of Christ or Mary, the mother of Jesus or any other Saint being worshipped.

**Idolatry of icons:** sacred paintings or a mosaic of God used for adoration and worship.

**Idolatry of pictures:** pictures of Jesus are prominent across the Christian world. It is prohibited to make a picture of Jesus and to bow down to it or to have an image of God in your mind.

**Idolatry of people:** It is prohibited to have a picture of someone on your wall and pray to it, bow down to it or worship it or use it to win favour and gain protection.

**Idolatry of false religions:**

**Hinduism/New Age**: Millions of gods are worshipped in the forms of statues and images. Some types believe in many incarnations of God.

**Buddhism**: images of different Buddha statues have been made across world and are worshipped or revered as sacred.

**Islam:** Although Islam claims to serve the true God and don't make images of God to bow down to and worship, they do bow down to a rock in Mecca and serve a false god. They don't recognize Jesus Christ as God or the Holy Spirit; therefore they don't serve the true God.

**Taoism:** This religion doesn't recognize the supremacy of an Infinite holy God who created all things. Adherents base their lives on a balance between evil and good, called yin/yan. Taoism is a form of dualism, which is contrary to sound doctrine.

**Bahai:** They believe that all religions serve the same God. This is false because Jesus said: "I am the way, the truth and the life. No one comes to the Father except through Me" (John 14:6 NKJV). See also: Acts 4:12; 1 John 5:12.

**Scripture to consider:** Jesus said: "But the hour is coming, and now is, when the true worshippers will worship the Father in spirit and truth: for the Father is seeking such to worship Him. God is Spirit: and those who worship Him must worship him in spirit and truth." (John 4:23,24 NKJV). "For we walk by faith, not by sight:" (2 Corinthians 5:7 ESV).

### 3. "You shall not take the name of the LORD your God in vain, for the LORD will not hold him guiltless who takes His name in vain" (Exodus 20:7 NKJV) Area: Speech

God teaches us in the third commandment that we must never misuse His Name, but always have respect for His Name and fear His Name and use His Name for His glory. The Bible reveals to us that God has many Names. "Immanuel" (Matthew 1:23 ESV), El Shaddai (God Almighty), El Elyon (God most High), "Prince of Peace" "Wonderful" (Isaiah 9:6 ESV), Jahwe Jireh "The Lord will provide"; (Genesis 22:14 ESV); Jahwe Rapha "The Lord, your Healer" (Exodus 15:26 ESV), Jahwe Rohi "The Lord is my shepherd" (Psalm 23:1 ESV) and so on. Jesus Christ is another Name of God which is so often misused and used in vain across the world. We see many times in the world or in programmes or films that people use the Name of Jesus or God as a stop-word. They don't use it with respect. They use it to express astonishment or surprise. God says in His Word that He will not hold him guiltless who misuses His Name. The Name of God (in Hebrew: Elohim) stands for who God is: His character. If we use God's Name out of context and without proper respect or reverence, we misrepresent God and therefore fall short of His glory.

**The Heidelberg Catechism** says of this commandment: That we, not only by cursing or perjury, but also by rash swearing, must not profane or abuse the Name of God; nor by silence or consent be partakers of these horrible sins in others; and briefly; that we use the holy Name of God no otherwise than with fear and reverence, so that He might be rightly confessed and worshipped by us, and be glorified in all our words and works.

It is written, "But the prophet who presumes to speak a word in My name, which I have not commanded him to speak, or who speaks in the name of other gods, that prophet shall die.' And if you say in your heart, 'How shall we know the word which the LORD has not spoken?'— when a prophet speaks in the name of the LORD, if the thing does not happen or come to pass, that is the thing which the LORD has not spoken; the prophet has spoken it presumptuously; you shall not be afraid of him" (Deuteronomy 18:20-22 NKJV). There are so many examples in our day of people who prophesy about this and that but then nothing happens. False prophecies being spoken are using the Name of God in vain. But this also relates to preachers who preach the Word of God but misinterpret passages of Scripture and twist His Word. We see this happening all over the world. Preachers take passages out of context and promise their hearers health, wealth and prosperity saying that the more we give to God the more He will be willing to bless us. By this practice, preachers enrich themselves. Many preachers of the Word of God think that godliness is a means to get rich (See 1 Timothy 6:5-8). Preachers use the Name of God to manipulate audiences for their own benefit and gain.

But these practices are not new. They were also prevalent in the prophet Jeremiah's day. God said the following to the prophets in Jeremiah's day: "I have heard what the prophets have said who prophesy lies in My name, saying, 'I have dreamed, I have dreamed!' How long will this be in the heart of the prophets who prophesy lies? Indeed they are prophets of the deceit of their own heart, who try to make My people forget My name by their dreams which everyone tells his neighbor, as their fathers forgot My name for Baal" (Jeremiah 23:25-27 NKJV). Children of God are also called prophets, but there is no more new, normative revelation, as the Scriptures of the Old and New Testament are complete and sufficient for salvation. Our function as New Testament prophets is to declare and proclaim the Word of God (Read 1 Peter 2:9; Mark 16:15; Ephesians 6:15) in the Bible and to expound the Word of God to those who need to hear it, not to add new revelation. Acts 19:10-17 gives us a good illustration of people who were not children of God but tried to use the Name of Jesus to cast out a demon, a stunt which backfired on them. The sons of Sceva misused the Name of God and because of that they suffered the consequences. In the Old Testament when one man used the Name of God as a swear word God judged him and he died (Read Leviticus 24:10-16).

God forbids the following sins by the third commandment:

**Profanity**: irreverent speech and talk; obscene language, swear words, dirty words, irreligious or irreverent behaviour.

**False prophecies:** speaking for God when God has not spoken. Predicting events that don't come to pass. Misinterpreting and misapplying the Word of God and twisting Scripture for selfish gain.

**Blasphemy:** irreverent talk about sacred things.

**Perjury:** the deliberate giving of false evidence while under oath.

It should be noted that all blasphemies can be forgiven and all words spoken against the Son of Man, who is Jesus; however, the blasphemy against the Holy Spirit cannot be forgiven (See Matthew 12:31). The blasphemy of the Holy Spirit is attributing Satan's work to the work of Jesus, knowing who Jesus is. That is what the Pharisees did in Jesus' day. Jesus said, "But I say to you that for every idle word men may speak, they will give account of it in the day of judgment. For by your words you will be justified, and by your words you will be condemned" (Matthew 12:36-37 NKJV). A person with a good heart brings forth honorable things, but a man with an evil heart brings forth detestable things (See Matthew 12:35). Paul the apostle commands us: "Let no corrupt word proceed out of your mouth, but what is good for necessary edification, that it may impart grace to the hearers" (Ephesians 4:29 NKJV). It is also written, "neither filthiness, nor foolish talking, nor coarse jesting, which are not fitting, but rather giving of thanks" (Ephesians 5:4 NKJV). Paul commands us: "Let your speech always be with grace, seasoned with salt, that you may know how you ought to answer each one." (Colossians 4:6 NKJV). Whatever we do as believers in Christ and whatever we say should reflect the character of God, therefore Paul commands us: "And whatever you do in word or deed, do all in the name of the Lord Jesus" (Colossians 3:17 NKJV).

**Truth to consider**: If we live ungodly lives as believers or if we speak in ways dishonouring to God, we bring insult on the Name of Christ and people will blaspheme God's Name because of us. Let us therefore walk and talk with wisdom, redeeming the time.

### 4. You shall keep the Sabbath holy/ Area: Time

The fourth commandment states: **"Remember the Sabbath day, to keep it holy. Six days you shall labor and do all your work, but the seventh day *is* the Sabbath of the LORD your God. *In it* you shall do no work: you, nor your son, nor your daughter, nor your male servant, nor your female servant, nor your cattle, nor your stranger who *is* within your gates. For *in* six days the LORD made the heavens and the earth, the sea, and all that *is* in them, and rested the seventh day. Therefore, the LORD blessed the Sabbath day and hallowed it."** (Exodus 20: 8-11 NKJV).

With this commandment God has given humans the privilege of working and of resting from our work. Doing work is not part of the curse which fell upon the human race because of their sin. God said: "let us make man in our image, after our likeness. And let them have dominion over the fish of the sea and over the birds of the heavens and over the livestock and over all the earth and over every creeping thing that creeps on the earth" (Genesis 1:26,27 ESV). God blessed the man and the woman and commanded them: "Be fruitful and multiply and fill the earth and subdue it and have dominion over … every living thing that moves on the earth" (Genesis 1:28 ESV). It is clear from these Scriptures and others (Psalm 8) that God made mankind to rule and to work on earth and have dominion over all living things of earth. Genesis 2:15 says the Lord took the man and put him in the garden of Eden to work it and keep it. We were made to work and to be God's representatives on this earth. Because of the fall of man, God said we will have difficulties and suffer when we work, for by the "sweat of your face" we shall eat bread (Genesis 3:19).

There is a rhythm in the created order and that is why God made the creation week so that we should follow Him in working and resting. We human beings are not God. We cannot work non-stop. We need sleep every day and we also need rest at the end of every week. God, however, does not need any sleep, because He is God (See Psalm 121). God made the Sabbath for man and not man for the Sabbath, as Jesus said. In Jesus' day the Pharisees often accused Him of doing good on the Sabbath and healing the lame and sick. Jesus, however, saw nothing wrong in doing good on the Sabbath (See Matthew 12:1-8). We should therefore not be legalistic about the Sabbath. We are allowed to do works of mercy and works of necessity on the Lord's Day (which replaced the Sabbath (See 1 Corinthians 16:2). If your car breaks down or someone breaks a leg or gets sick or you have any crisis, it is allowed according to the law of love to help those in need and in any crisis. Therefore, people working as doctors (for example) or vets or in the police or in the army, can do their duties on the Lord's Day. Paul commanded the believers in Ephesians 4:28, "Let him who stole steal no longer, but rather let him labor, working with his hands what is good, that he may have something to give him who has need" (Ephesians 4:28 NKJV). Paul also reprimanded the believers saying, "…we commanded you this: If anyone will not work, neither shall he eat. For we hear that there are some who walk among you in a disorderly manner, not working at all, but are busybodies... we command and exhort through our Lord Jesus Christ that they work in quietness and eat their own bread" (II Thessalonians 3:10-12 NKJV).

The **Heidelberg Catechism** says the following of this commandment:

"First, the ministry of the gospel and the schools be maintained and that I, especially on the Sabbath, that is the day of rest, diligently frequent the church of God to hear His word, to use His sacraments, publicly to call upon the Lord, and contribute to the relief of the poor, as becomes a Christian. Secondly, that all the days of my life I cease from my evil works, and yield myself to the Lord, to work by the Holy Spirit in me, and thus begin in this life the eternal Sabbath."

Many Christians are contentious about whether the day of rest should be on a Sunday or on Saturday. They say the people of God in the Old Testament rested on the Saturday. This is true, but it is clear from the New Testament writings (Read 1 Corinthians 16:2; Acts 20:7; Revelation 1:10) and from the early Christian fathers, that the Lord's day was the day when the Christians came together and broke bread and stored up money and other items for the poor. Because Jesus Christ rose from the dead on the first day of the week and because God started His new work of redeeming people by Christ, or the new creation, on Sunday, Sunday was the obvious day to come together and celebrate and hear the Word of God preached. Some Christians regard all days as the same as Paul said (See Romans 14:5,6) and some believe keeping the Sabbath is part of the Old Covenant (See Colossians 2:16,17). It is true the Sabbaths in the Old Testament were the shadow of things to come. To be united to Christ is the substance of the spiritual life and in Him we rest of our evil deeds. However, we are still in this body and this body gets tired and sleepy and sick and old, therefore, let us not be wiser than God but come to Jesus Christ at the appointed times to be refreshed by the Word of God and the fellowship of the brethren (See Acts 2:42,46).

Sins forbidden by the fourth commandment:

**Desecration of the Lord's day**: forsaking the assembling of the brethren (Read Hebrews 10:25; 3:13). Going on with normal work and not setting time aside for fellowship with other believers and for hearing the Word of God.

**Laziness:** laziness is condemned by many texts (Read Proverbs 6:6-11) in the Bible because we were made in the image of God and to represent Him on the earth. If we don't work we live irresponsibly and selfishly. We were made to work. Work is love in action.

**Workaholism:** working without taking necessary rest and time of refreshment in the Word of God. Workaholism is a form of pride. When we seek God and His kingdom first God will give us what we need. We don't have to work in a way thinking our livelihood depends on ourselves. The reason God gave the Sabbaths to old Israel and the seventh year of rest was so that they would depend and trust in Him.

**Scriptures to consider:** Jesus said "Come to Me, all you who labor and are heavy laden, and I will give you rest. Take My yoke upon you and learn from Me, for I am gentle and lowly in heart, and you will find rest for your souls. For My yoke is easy and My burden is light" (Matthew 11:28-30 NKJV). We cannot rest rightly unless we work. And when we work with God and take His yoke upon us we will enter eternal rest.

> 5. **"Honor your father and your mother, that your days may be long upon the land which the LORD your God is giving you" (Exodus 20:12 NKJV) Area: Authority**

God commands us in the fifth commandment to have the utmost respect for our parents, whether they are believers in God or not, whether they conduct themselves in shameful and sinful ways or not, whether they are worthy of our honour and respect or not. And this is the only commandment with a promise, "that your days may be long upon the land which the Lord your God is giving you" (Exodus 20:12 NKJV). Now the first meaning of this commandment is that God promised the

Israelites long lives in the land of Israel if they obeyed Him. But this commandment and the promise certainly concern Christian believers as well: they will inherit the new heavens and the new earth (See Revelation 21:1,2,7). And Jesus said, "blessed are the meek, for they shall inherit the earth" (Matthew 5:5 ESV). You may wonder how the words: "the meek" connect to honouring and respecting your father and mother. The answer is that the proud always trust in themselves and think they don't need advice and counsel, but the humble and meek in heart submit to authority. God commands: "Children, obey your parents in the Lord, for this is right" (Ephesians 6:1 ESV). If your parents demand of you to do something contrary to God's Word, you should not obey them. For example, if they ask you to steal for them or disrespect your teachers or live a sinful life, then it is right to disobey them! Even your parents can abuse their authority before God, and only then it is lawful to disobey them.

This commandment doesn't only refer to submitting to authority in your own household, to your mother and father, but also to authority in the church (the people of God) and civil authority, in government. The humble in heart obey and submit to authority because they recognize that all authority is from God. That is what Paul commanded in the letter to the Romans: "Let every soul be subject to the governing authorities. For there is no authority except from God, and the authorities that exist are appointed by God. Therefore whoever resists the authority resists the ordinance of God, and those who resist will bring judgment on themselves" (Romans 13:1-2 NKJV). Believers in God should therefore pay, "...taxes to whom taxes are owed, revenue to whom revenue is owed, respect to whom respect is owed" (Romans 13:7 ESV; See also 1 Peter 2:13,14) as far as the government of the particular country is obeying everything according to the constitution (if the country is governed by a constitution). Christians should always obey traffic laws, teenagers and children and young adults should, therefore, obey and submit to their teachers and lecturers as far as they do things that are in accordance with God's commandments. We know that many dictatorships and oppressive regimes have abused the authority that they have received from God, for example in Communist countries in Eastern Europe. The same applied to China and Russia in the twentieth century, and throughout the past two millennia to countries that are ruled by Islam and Sharia law. But even in these countries we should only in extreme cases take up arms to overthrow them. In those countries where the governments misuse their authority we should remember God commands, "if possible, so far as it depends on you, live peaceably with all. Beloved, never avenge yourselves, but leave it to the wrath of God, for it is written, "Vengeance is mine, I will repay, says the Lord" (Romans 12:18,19 ESV). Every person who has ever lived will stand before God and give account of the lives they have lived (See Romans 2:16; Revelation 20:11-15). Even today in so called "free countries" abortion on demand is legal, homosexual marriages, prostitution and sexual immorality are legal. This doesn't mean that God approves of sin, nor that those people who participate in these deeds will not be judged. It would be lawful to resist tyranny in a country if what is happening in the country goes against international law. The problem is that the international community is not consistent in executing justice and labelling acts as crimes against humanity.

In church, we also are to be subject to one another and submit ourselves to those who have authority over us (See Hebrews 13:17). The younger should be subject to the elders in the church and to those who are older. Everybody should be subject to one another (Read 1 Peter 5:1-6). But we should not only be subject to those in our current local church family but to the church fathers throughout all ages. Local churches can teach error and lead their flocks on the wrong paths. That is why we should learn from the church and family of God of all ages. People like Athanasius, Augustine, Martin Luther, Charles Spurgeon, Jonathan Edwards, R.C. Sproul and many others have rediscovered the central teachings of the Word of God, which we should submit to. And then of course there are the prophets and apostles who were given the infallible, trustworthy words of God (See 2 Timothy 3:26; 2 Peter 1:20,21) found in the Old and New Testaments, which we should submit to.

The **Heidelberg Catechism** requires the following concerning this commandment: "That I show all honour, love and fidelity, to my father and mother and all in authority over me, and submit myself to their good

85

instruction and correction, with due obedience and so patiently bear with their weaknesses and infirmities, since it pleases God to govern us by their hand."

God forbids the following sins by this command:

**Disobedience:** not obeying and submitting to the authorities over you (family, church, employers, and government).

**Disrespect:** lack of respect and showing disregard, ignoring authority

**Dishonour:** disgrace, not honouring and showing respect

**Cheekiness:** Cheerful show of disrespect

If we are working in a company or an organization, or for the government or a non-profit organization, this command implies that we also obey our employers and give them due respect (Read Ephesians 6:5-9; 1 Peter 2:13). And above all we ought to submit to the King and Ruler of all who reigns over the church, the government and our families; He is God (See Ephesians 1:20-22; 1 Peter 3:22). Whenever there is a conflict between what God requires and God's revealed Word, and what anyone tells you in the church, your family, the government or an employer we must always obey God. Obeying God according to righteousness was the example of the apostles (Read Acts 5:29).

**Scriptures to consider:** "The words of the wise are as goads, and as nails firmly fixed are the collected sayings; they are given by one Shepherd" (Ecclesiastes 12:11 ESV). "Listen to counsel, and receive instruction, that you may be wise in your latter days" (Proverbs 19:20 NKJV).

### 6. "You shall not murder" (Exodus 20:13 NKJV) Area: Life

There is a big difference between killing someone and murdering someone. The former is not necessarily sin, but the latter is always a sin. God for example kills people and it is not a sin. He gives life and He takes a life. It is written, "The Lord kills and brings to life; he brings down to Sheol and raises up" (1 Samuel 2:6 ESV). Also God declares: "See now that I, even I, am He, and there is no god beside Me; I kill and make alive; I wound, and I heal" (Deuteronomy 32:39 ESV). God never murders anyone; murder is taking an innocent life. We all have sinned and are therefore deserving of death (Read Romans 6:23; Ezekiel 18:20) and when God takes our lives He has done no evil. But when we take an innocent life and when we plan to take a life by malicious intent it is evil; as the Bible says, "Whoever sheds the blood of man, by man shall his blood be shed, for God made man in his own image" (Genesis 9:6 ESV). Life is precious in God's sight and we should value life because we were made in God's image. God, "...hates hands that shed innocent blood" (Proverbs 6:17 ESV). But there is a time for everything. There is "a time to kill, and a time to heal" (Ecclesiastes 3:3 ESV). God has given the governing authorities the right to execute murderers and those who deserve death. God declares that the governing authorities do not bear the sword in vain, for "he is the servant of God, an avenger who carries out God's wrath on the wrongdoer" (Romans 13:4 ESV). To protect and defend your life and kill when a burglar or a murderer wants to take your life or the life of a family member is not sin (See Exodus 22:2).

God commands us in the sixth commandment to protect the sanctity of life, protect innocent life, defend people who are vulnerable and weak and sick against evil people, evil governments, evil organizations, evil and malicious societies and terrorists. God commands: "Deliver those who are drawn toward death, And hold back those stumbling to the slaughter. If you say, "Surely we did not know this," Does not He who weighs the hearts consider it? He who keeps your soul, does He not know it? And will He not render to each man according to his deeds?" (Proberbs 24:11-12 NKJV). This command does not only imply that we must rescue unborn babies in their mothers' wombs, since life begins at conception (See Psalm 139:13-16), and to speak up for those who cannot speak up for themselves (Read Proverbs 31:8), but also that we warn the wicked who are on their way to hell and eternal destruction (Read Ezekiel 3:18-21). If we don't warn the wicked of their evil way and they die, we are also guilty. This means that we should share the gospel and proclaim the only way of salvation (Read John 3:16; Acts 4:12; Mark 16:15) with as many people as possible. Would it not be reckoned as hate towards our neighbours if we keep silent about the only way to escape the horrors of hell and the wrath to come? God commanded us not only to love Him with all our hearts but also to love our neighbour as ourselves (Read Matthew 22:36-39) and even to "love your enemies" (Matthew 5:44 ESV).

The **Heidelberg Catechism** goes further and says what God requires by this commandment: That neither in thoughts, nor words, nor gestures, much less in deeds, I dishonour, hate, wound, or kill my neighbour, by myself or by another, but that I lay aside all desire for revenge, also, that I hurt not myself, nor willingly expose myself to danger. Wherefore also the magistrate is armed with the sword to prevent murder. In forbidding murder, God teaches us that He abhors the causes thereof such as envy, hatred, anger, and the desire for revenge; and that He accounts all of these as murder.

The Bible states: "Whoever hates his brother is a murderer, and you know that no murderer has eternal life abiding in him" (1 John 3:15 NKJV). Jesus also said: "whoever is angry with his brother without a cause shall be in danger of the judgment... whoever says, "You fool", shall be in danger of hell fire" (Matthew 5:22 NKJV). There is something like righteous anger towards sin and evil, but we should always be careful not to avenge ourselves on people. Vengeance belongs to God (Read Romans 12:19 ESV). We are, however, commanded to hate evil and sin (Read Romans 12:9; Psalm 97:10; Proverbs 8:13), and to cast away unforgiveness and bitterness against people (Read Hebrews 12:15; Matthew 18:21-35). Jesus went so far as to say: "...but if you do not forgive others their trespasses, neither will your Father forgive your trespasses" (Matthew 6:15 ESV). Only by the presence and power of the Holy Spirit can we forgive as God forgives, therefore let us always come to God to be filled with His Spirit (Read Ephesians 5:18).

Sins forbidden by this commandment:

**Murder:** intentional unlawful killing, the premeditated malicious taking of a life.

**Suicide:** the intentional killing of oneself; an act destructive of one's own interests.

**Abortion:** the premature expulsion of a foetus from the womb, an operation to cause this.

**Euthanasia:** bringing about an easy death to end suffering, through injection or detracting medical machinery or otherwise.

**Hate towards people and enemies:** extreme dislike or enmity

**Keeping the gospel to oneself:** not sharing the good news of salvation accomplished through Jesus Christ when the opportunity arises. Also, not making use of means to share the gospel with those who need it.

**Unforgiveness:** not forgiving a wrongdoing by another person/ people.

**Bitterness:** harbouring a grudge against someone, unwilling to forgive someone and hatred towards that person. Harbouring resentment towards someone.

**Unrighteous anger:** Anger which is not justifiable by God's law and nature.

**Jealousy and envy:** resentment towards a rival; discontent arising from another's possessions or success.

**Assaulting someone:** attacking someone to do harm.

**Putting oneself in unnecessary danger:** e.g. driving too fast in public areas, swimming in shark-infested waters, etc.

**Malice:** desire to harm others

**Slander:** a false statement uttered maliciously that damages or ruins a person's reputation.

**Truths and Scripture to consider**: an unwillingness to protect and care for and nurture other human beings is to hate people. God states: "...to him who knows to do good and does not do it, to him it is sin" (James 4:17 NKJV). Unwillingness to reflect God's holy and loving character to one's neighbour and misrepresenting God on earth will result in everlasting condemnation (Read Matthew 25:31-46).

### 7. **"You shall not commit adultery"** (Exodus 20:14 NKJV)
**Area: Love**

We live in an age where sexual sins pollute our communities. With this command God intends to protect the sanctity of marriage. In the beginning when God made man and woman the Bible states the following: "...God created man in his own image….male and female he created them. And God blessed them. And God said to them, "Be fruitful and multiply and fill the earth" (Genesis 1:27,28 ESV). And after God created man He said: "It is not good that man should be alone; I will make a helper fit for him" (Genesis 2:18 ESV). And after He made the woman He said: "Therefore a man shall leave his father and his mother and hold fast to his wife, and they shall become one flesh" (Genesis 2:24 ESV). God instituted marriage and He instituted sex for mankind to enjoy within the bond of one man and one woman in the covenant of marriage. The world and the sin of mankind have, however, perverted and polluted the covenant of marriage ever since. We see today that prostitution and promiscuity, fornication, adultery, homosexuality and pornography are freely being practiced and made legal all throughout the world. Ecclesiastes 3:11 says God has made everything beautiful in its time, but man has corrupted what God has made. God knows that "every intention of the thoughts of his heart was only evil continually" (Genesis 6:5 ESV). This was true of mankind before and this is still true today.

There are many passages in Scripture that warn us to flee from sexual immorality. Our bodies are supposed to be temples of the Holy Spirit. God has made our bodies not for sexual immorality but for Him (Read 1 Corinthians 6:12-19). With this command God sanctions **only** sexual activity between one woman and one man in the bond of marriage. All other sexual activity and desires for sex are forbidden. God commands us: "Flee from sexual immorality" (1 Corinthains 6:18 ESV). God commands us, "So flee youthful passions and pursue righteousness, faith, love, and peace, along with those who call on the Lord from a pure heart" (2 Timothy 2:22 ESV). To have a blessed marriage and live a God-honouring life, God wants us to have a pure heart. Jesus said: "Blessed are the pure in heart, for they shall see God" (Matthew 5:8 ESV). We will be happy when we strive for holiness in regard to sexuality. God warns us in His Word that, "….neither the sexually immoral, nor idolaters, nor adulterers, nor men who practice homosexuality...will inherit the kingdom of God" (1 Corinthians 6:9-10 ESV). Jesus went so far as to say: "...that whoever looks at a woman to lust for her has already committed adultery with her in his heart" (Matthew 5:28 NKJV). If that is how God sees adultery then we have all fallen short and broken God's law numerous times. And God said, "Marriage is honorable among all, and the bed undefiled; but fornicators and adulterers God will judge" (Hebrews 13:4 NKJV).

The **Heidelberg Catechism** tells us what this commandment teaches:

That all uncleanness is accursed by God, and that therefore we must with all our hearts detest the same, and live chastely and temperately, whether in holy wedlock or in single life. Since both body and soul are temples of the Holy Spirit, He commands us to preserve them pure and holy; therefore, He forbids all unchaste actions, gestures, words, thoughts and desires, and whatever can entice men thereto.

If we take this explanation to heart we see that many things in our communities are evil in God's sight. Sexually explicit billboards, advertisements, sexual innuendo in movies and programs etc. are all forbidden by God. In Leviticus 18:1-30 and 20:10-20 God lists many sexual sins that are still applicable for us to flee from and to abhor.

The following sins are forbidden by this commandment:

**Adultery:** having sexual intercourse with someone who is not your husband or wife

**Fornication:** having sexual intercourse while unmarried

**Promiscuity:** having sexual relations with many people

**Pornography:** writings, pictures or videos intended to stimulate erotic feelings by portraying sexual activity.

**Prostitution:** a woman, man, teenager or child who offers sexual intercourse for payment

**Sexual lust:** intense sexual desire

**Homosexuality and homosexual behaviour:** sexual attraction to people of the same sex; having sexual intercourse with someone of the same sex.

**Incest:** sexual intercourse between very closely related people, in your family e.g. with a father, daughter, uncle, niece, cousin, grandfather.

**Bestiality:** having sexual intercourse with animals

**Voyeurism:** getting pleasure from watching others having sex or undressing e.g. on Television or the Internet or in real life.

**Exhibitionism:** undressing yourself in front of other people to attract attention to yourself and stimulate sexual desire.

**Orgies:** a wild party, unrestrained sexual activity

**Sex with minors:** Adults having sex with children

**Molestation:** Attack or interfere sexually with another person

**Rape:** having sexual intercourse with someone without his/her consent or permission.

**Masturbation:** stimulation of the genitals with the hand.

**Immodesty:** dressing in a way that would stimulate sexual desire from another. Especially regarding women.

**Sexually provocative advertisements:** advertisements that are intended to stimulate sexual desire e.g. on Billboards, in magazines, newspapers, in the cinemas, on television, etc.

**Sexual immorality:** includes all sexual activity except sex within the bond of marriage between one man and one woman.

**Flirting**: behave in a frivolous and amorous (showing sexual love) way towards someone who is not your husband or wife

God said in 1 Thessalonians 4:3-8, "For this is the will of God, your sanctification: that you should abstain from sexual immorality; that each one of you should know how to control his own body in holiness and honour, not in the passion of lust as the Gentiles do who do not know God….For God has not called us to impurity, but in holiness. Therefore, whoever disregards this, disregards not man but God, who gives his Holy Spirit to you" (1 Thessalonians 4:3-5,7 ESV).

**Reality to consider**: Engaging in sexual immorality can result in getting one of over 50 sexually transmitted diseases (e.g. contracting HIV/AIDS), some which are incurable. God says: "for the one who sows to his own flesh will from the flesh reap corruption" (Galatians 6:8 ESV).

### 8. "You shall not steal" (Exodus 20:15 NKJV) Area: Property

The eight and tenth commandments overlap in some areas. The reason why people steal and why they covet is because of greed and envy. The reason people steal and desire things they shouldn't is because they are not content with the things God has given them. This commandment also presupposes the privilege and right people have to own property and to have possessions. If we are content with the things God has given us, whether they are many things or few, whether we are poor or rich, we will benefit much. 1 Timothy 6:6 states: "Godliness with contentment is great gain. For we brought nothing into this world, and it is certain that we can carry nothing out. Having food and clothing let us be therefore be content." To be content with what you have means to be thankful to God and satisfied with the things He has given you. God commands: "Keep your life free from the love of money, and be content with what you have, for He has said: 'I will never leave you nor forsake you.' So, we can confidently say, 'The Lord is my helper, I will not fear, what can man do to me?'" (Hebrews 13:5,6 ESV). If our trust is in God and if we seek His kingdom and righteousness, God will give us the things we need in due time. People are tempted to steal many times because they don't believe they have what they need at the current time. Because of unbelief in God's providence, people are discontented, dissatisfied and unthankful.

Jesus was a poor man in the world's eyes, yet He owned the universe.

If we are children of God the Bible says that we are rich because we have the blessed Holy Spirit within us and because God has prepared for us an inheritance in heaven which is imperishable, unfading and incorruptible (See Ephesians 1:12-14; 1 Peter 1:4). Jesus told us, "... lay up for yourselves treasures in heaven, where neither moth nor rust destroys and where thieves do not break in and steal" (Matthew 6:20 ESV). God said these remarkable words about believers: "...all things are yours, whether Paul or Apollos or Peter or the world or life or death or the present or the future – all are yours, and you are Christ's, and Christ is God's" (1 Corinthians 3:21-23 ESV). If we have this vision of God, we would not envy and steal and desire other people's possessions, because all belongs to God. The Lord states: "The earth is the Lord's and the fullness thereof, the world and those who dwell therein." (Psalm 24:1 ESV). If God owns everything and we are His children by faith in the Holy Spirit then all belongs to us as well. That doesn't mean you can take things left, right and centre that don't belong to you – that would be theft – but spiritually everything that is God's is ours as well. Moreover, the Bible makes it clear that we are stewards of the things God has given us. Everything God has given to us must be used, not selfishly, but for His glory, for the extension of God's kingdom and for the good of the church (Read Matthew 25:14-31; Matthew 21:33-43; Luke 16:9-12). Pride in one's own abilities and living independently from God as well as idolatry in all its facets, are also forms of theft, because they rob God of the glory that is due to Him.

The **Heidelberg Catechism** says the following:

God forbids not only those thefts and robberies which are punishable by the magistrate; but He comprehends under the name theft all wicked tricks and devices, whereby we design to appropriate to ourselves the goods which belong to our neighbour; whether it be by force, or under the appearance of right, as by unjust weights, measures, fraudulent merchandise, false coins, usury, or by any other way forbidden by God, as all covetousness, and abuse and waste of His gifts. Also, God requires that I promote the advantage of my neighbour in every instance I can or may, and deal with him as I desire to be dealt with by others; further also that I faithfully labour, so that I may be able to relieve the needy.

The following sins are forbidden by this commandment:

**Theft:** taking something that doesn't belong to you or is not rightfully yours; take dishonestly.

**Fraud:** criminal deception, a dishonest trick to get what is not rightfully yours.

**Greed:** excessive desire for food, wealth or possessions

**Laziness:** unwilling to work, doing little work

**Socialism and communism:** a political and economic system whereby resources, industries and transport should be owned and managed by the state. Communism and socialism are legalized theft. Socialism is institutionalized envy.

**Vandalism:** wilfully damaging of property and destroying property

**Wastefulness:** use something, or something used extravagantly or without adequate result; fail to use.

**Kleptomania:** a compulsive desire to steal

**Gambling:** play games of chance for money; risk in hope of gain

**Discontent:** not content and satisfied with what you have

**Ungratefulness**: complaining, not thanking God and man for the things that you have and the abilities, talents and opportunities that God has given you

**Usury:** the lending of money at excessive high rates of interest.

**Adultery:** taking someone else's wife to be your own

**Idolatry**: taking glory and honour for yourself or giving it to someone or something instead of what is rightfully God's; robbing God

**Tax evasion**: not paying the state what is rightfully theirs.

--The Bible makes it clear: "Let the thief no longer steal, but rather let him labour, doing honest work with his own hands, so that he may have something to share with those in need" (Ephesians 4:28 ESV). Concerning gambling and laziness the Word of God says, "the desire of the sluggard kills him because his hands refuse to labour" (Proverbs 21:25 ESV). God states: "wealth gained hastily will dwindle, but whoever gathers little by little will increase it" (Proverbs 13:11 ESV). God states: "A man with an evil eye hastens after riches, and does not consider that poverty will come upon him" (Proverbs 28:22 NKJV).

**Truth and Scripture to consider:** We are stewards of God's grace and possessions in this world. Jesus said: "…make for yourselves friends by means of unrighteous wealth, so when it fails, they may receive you into eternal dwellings. One who is faithful in a very little is also faithful in much…If you then have not been faithful in unrighteous wealth, who will entrust to you the true riches?" (Luke 16:9-11 ESV). We are commanded by God to use money to win people for the kingdom.

## 9. "You shall not give false testimony of your neighbour" (Exodus 20:16 NKJV) / Area: Truth

The Word of God makes it very clear that God is the God of truth. God cannot tell a lie or be deceitful. He cannot give false information about Himself and He cannot lie when He speaks about human beings or the world we live in (Read Titus 1:2). God has promised believers in Christ eternal life and that is what believers will have! The fact that God cannot lie and always speaks the truth and always reveals the truth means that we can trust Him, His character and His promises in the Word of God, which is still relevant for us today. That is also the reason the Word of God is called the Word of truth (See Ephesians 1:13; Colossians 1:5; James 1:15) through which we are born again by the Spirit of God and inherit eternal life. The word of God states: "God is not man, that he should lie, or a son of man that he should change his mind" (Numbers 23:19 ESV). Jesus is called "the way, and the truth and the life" (John 14:6 ESV) and the Spirit of God is called the "Spirit of truth" (John 14:17 ESV) who leads believers into the truth about themselves, the world, and about God. When we say that God is the God of truth we mean that there is nothing false in His being, in what He says and does. He has not revealed exhaustively things about Himself (Read Deuteronomy 29:29), but in the Bible, He has revealed to us what He has purposed for mankind, so that we may be saved from our sins, from His wrath, and so that we may know how we can live, God-pleasing, God-honouring and righteous lives on earth. God is love and the Bible says love "rejoices with the truth" (1 Corinthians 13:6 ESV).

The Bible reveals that, "if we say that we have no sin, we deceive ourselves, and the truth is not in us. If we confess our sins, he is faithful and just to forgive us our sins, and to cleanse us from all unrighteousness. If we say that we have not sinned, we make him a liar, and the word is not in us" (1 John 1:8-10 ESV). The Bible says "for all have sinned and fall short of the glory of God" (Romans 3:23 NKJV). This commandment helps us to be honest about ourselves before God and to speak the truth with others and with God. We are not people who hide things and who keep things in darkness. We walk in the light as God is in the light (See

1 John 1:7). If we want to represent God faithfully in this earth we ought to speak the truth. The Bible states: "The truthful lip shall be established forever, but a lying tongue is but for a moment" (Proverbs 12:19 NKJV). The Bible says, "...that the unbelieving, abominable, murderers, sexually immoral, sorcerers, idolaters, and all liars shall have their part in the lake which burns with fire and brimstone, which is the second death" (Revelation 21:8 NKJV). Liars will not inherit the kingdom of God. God hates lying (See Proverbs 6:6-19) because it misrepresents Him. The devil is called the father of lies (See John 8:44) and that is why there are so many false religions and cults in this world. The devil cannot speak the truth; there is no truth in him. And those who love to tell lies, fibs, half-truths, and to deceive people and exaggerate, are followers of the evil one.

This command teaches us not only to avoid and hate deception and lies but to always speak the truth, love the truth, rejoice in the truth and protect the reputation of our neighbours and fellow human beings. With this command we should promote and stand for what is right and true in society, in our churches, in politics and in every sphere of society. We are to uphold the good name of our neighbours and shun both slander and gossiping about our neighbours. God commands: "to speak evil of no one" (Titus 3:2 NKJV). That doesn't mean we shouldn't expose the works of darkness when the opportunity arises (Read Ephesians 5:11). Speaking the truth in an unloving way can hurt a person, therefore we are commanded to be "speaking the truth in love" (Ephesians 4:15 NKJV). It is sometimes better to keep silent (See Ecclesiastes 3:7) but when love demands it, we should confront people if it would result in the coming of God's kingdom and the establishing of the kingdom of truth (Read Proverbs 27:5).

The **Heidelberg Catechism** says the following about this commandment: "That I bear false witness against no man nor falsify any man's words, that I be no backbiter, nor slanderer, that I do not judge, nor join in condemning any man rashly or unheard, but that I avoid all sorts of lies and deceit as the proper works of the devil, unless I would bring down upon me the wrath of God; likewise, that in judgement and all other dealings I love the truth, speak it uprightly and confess it; also that I defend and promote, as much as I am able, the honor and good character of my neighbor."

Sins forbidden by this command include:

**Lies:** a statement the speaker knows to be untrue

**White lies:** a harmless or trivial lie, especially one told to avoid hurting someone's feelings; a lie told to be polite or to stop someone from being upset

**Dishonesty:** not being honest and truthful

**Deceit:** cause to believe something that is not true

**Slander:** a false statement uttered maliciously that damages a person's reputation; the crime of uttering this.

**Gossip:** casual talk about other people's affairs which puts someone in a negative light

**Perjury:** deliberate giving of false evidence while under oath; this evidence

**Backbiting:** spiteful talk (malicious desire to hurt or annoy someone)

**Character defamation:** attack the good reputation of someone

**Character assassination:** destroying someone's character by giving false information to the public and exaggerating their mistakes

**Exaggeration:** make something seem greater than it really is

**Judge rashly and condemning people in your heart**

Jesus told us, "Judge not, and you shall not be judged. Condemn not, and you shall not be condemned. Forgive, and you will be forgiven" (Luke 6:37 NKJV). Jesus told us to forgive because it would be the evidence that we have been forgiven. Man knows the extent of evil if he looks at himself in the mirror of God's law. If any man receives Christ's forgiveness and realizes how many sins have been forgiven him it would be hard to condemn any other person, because he knows the extent of evil in his own heart that God forgave him in Christ Jesus.

**Scripture to consider**: "These six things the LORD hates, yes seven are an abomination to Him: a proud look, A lying tongue, hands that shed innocent blood, a heart that devises wicked plans, feet that are swift in running to evil, a false witness who speaks lies, and one who sows discord among brethren" (Proverbs 6:16-19 NKJV).

> **10. "You shall not covet your neighbor's house; you shall not covet your neighbor's wife, nor his male servant, nor his female servant, nor his ox, nor his donkey, nor anything that is your neighbor's" (Exodus 20:17 NKJV)/ Area: conscience**

Covetousness is a root sin. Covetousness means to desire something that belongs to someone else. Covetousness is therefore not being content and happy and satisfied and thankful for the things that God has given you. The greatest thing God has ever given mankind is His Son Jesus Christ (See Romans 8:32) when He became a human being. Because God gave His only begotten Son (Read John 3:16) to this world we can have everlasting life in the Holy Spirit. Jesus said to His disciples: "if you then, being evil, know how to give good gifts to your children, how much more will your Father who is in heaven give good things to those who ask Him!" (Matthew 7:11 NKJV). God has given us His Son, Jesus Christ, so that He can give us His best, Himself, the Holy Spirit (See John 14:16,17). If you know that God has given you His best, Himself, and if you have truly received the Holy Spirit you will be dissatisfied with all the other things the world offers. It is true that God gives us many good things that are not God, good things, like a wife or children, or a husband, or education or food and water and houses and good clothes, and all these things are good, but they are not the best. God is the best. We can thank God and we should thank and praise God for all the other good things He gives us richly to enjoy (See 1 Timothy 6:17). We should be deeply thankful for "every good and every perfect gift" (James 1:17 NKJV) that is from above but it should never compete with the greatest Treasure, who is God. When you don't realize this and when you are not satisfied with all that God was, is and will be for us in Christ Jesus and the Holy Spirit, covetousness is inevitable.

If we have this perspective on God's all-sufficiency, then we will be content with the things God gives us, whether they are few and of little monetary value or whether they are of much monetary value. Paul said: "Now godliness with contentment is great gain. For we brought nothing into this world, and it is certain we can carry nothing out. And having food and clothing, with these we shall be content" (1 Timothy 6:6-8 NKJV). Covetousness is idolatry (See Ephesians 5:5; Colossians 3:5) because it makes God's *gifts* instead of Himself our hope and trust and treasure. That is why Jesus said we cannot serve God and Mammon (Money) at the same time. We will either love the one or the other more. And if our hope and trust is in what money can buy or in God's gifts we will never be satisfied, because when will enough things be enough? As Augustine said: "our hearts are restless until we find rest in God." We may add: Our hearts are dissatisfied until it is satisfied with God in Christ Jesus. When we look to God and treasure Him above all and love Him above all, then we use the gifts of God and the things God gives us for His glory and not for being content. The glitter and applause of the world cannot eternally satisfy our spiritual thirst. We were made to be satisfied with God alone and unless you have come to rest in God's all-sufficient, all satisfying presence you will wander in the world after things, more things, other people's husbands or wives or more money or fame or prestige or success and it will eventually leave you empty, disillusioned and lost.

This commandment not only forbids unlawful desire of what mankind possesses but also of another man's achievements, his intelligence, his talents, his opportunities and his unique personality. This command helps us to be content with the unique people God has made us to be, and not to compare ourselves with one another (Read 2 Corinthians 10:12; Galatians 6:4-5), and to covet and desire to be more like Jesus Christ. That kind of desiring and coveting is not sinful but commanded. The will of God is that, "we all come to the unity of the faith and of the knowledge of the Son of God, to a perfect man, to the measure of the stature of the fullness of Christ" (Ephesians 4:13 NKJV).

The **Heidelberg Catechism** says the following about this commandment: "That even the smallest inclination or thought contrary to any of God's commandments never rise in our hearts; but that at all times we hate sin with our whole heart, and delight in all righteousness." Question 114 goes further and says: even the holiest men, while in this life, have only a small beginning of this obedience, yet so that with a sincere resolution they begin to live, not only according to some, but all the commandments of God.

The Bible is replete with commandments to give thanks to God for who He is, what He has done and what good gifts He has given us (See 1 Thessalonians 5:17; Philippians 4:5-7; Colossians 4:2; Psalm 92:1; Psalm 107:1). As Paul said: ""For who makes you differ from another? And what do you have that you did not receive? Now if you did indeed receive it, why do you boast as if you had not received it?"(1 Corinthians 4:7 NKJV). If it is true that all we own, all we have, all our gifts and talents and abilities and resources and opportunities are given to us from God we ought to be the most thankful of all! Let us make it a habit to count our blessings one by one.

The following sins are forbidden by this commandment:

**Covetousness:** desiring things belonging to another person

**Greed:** excessive desire for food or wealth or possessions

**Discontent:** dissatisfaction with what God has given you

**Idolatry:** worship of idols (an image or person or thing worshipped other than God); not having God uppermost in your affections

**Jealousy:** resentful towards a rival for what he owns, what he has accomplished, what he knows, his successes or his abilities

**Envy:** discontentment aroused by another's possessions or success.

**Socialism:** a political and economic theory that resources, industries, and transport should be owned and managed by the state. Socialism is institutionalized envy.

**Love of money:** making money the thing you trust in

**Unthankfulness:** not being thankful and grateful

**Grumbling:** complaining in a bad-tempered way

**Complaining**: say one is dissatisfied; say one is suffering from pain

**Scripture to consider**: "But fornication and all uncleanness or covetousness, let it not even be named among you, as is fitting for saints; neither filthiness, nor foolish talking, nor coarse jesting, which are not fitting, but rather giving of thanks" (Ephesians 5:3-4 NKJV).

# CONCLUSION

We said in the beginning that the law of God, specifically the Ten Commandments have three purposes or functions:

The first is to show the character of God (See Romans 7:7) and the sinfulness of man (See Romans 3:19,20), making him hopeless and helpless resulting in him standing guilty before God, needing a Saviour (See Galatians 3:24).

Secondly, they also help to restrain evil in society and instil the fear of God, and thirdly, they show us how to live a righteous and God-pleasing life unto God (Read Matthew 22:36-40; Romans 13:8-10).

James also said these shocking words: "For whoever shall keep the whole law and yet stumble in one point, he is guilty of all" (James 2:10 NKJV). For many years I thought this statement was harsh but thinking about it more and about the Ten Commandments I see how true it is. Let us say for example you steal something. In doing that you dishonour God, misrepresent Him and blaspheme His Name.

In other words you become guilty of not working as you should, breaking the first four commandments. By taking from someone else you hate your neighbour; you show yourself greedy; you steal; covetousness drives you, and so on. Every sin committed dishonours your neighbour and results in misrepresenting and dishonouring God; every sin that a person commits demonstrates that he/she hates God and his/her neighbour. If we look deep into the law of God we see that we all deserve His wrath thousands of times.

I encourage you to pray with David as you go through each commandment: "Search me, O God, and know my heart; Try me, and know my anxieties; And see if there is any wicked way in me, And lead me in the way everlasting" (Psalms 139:23-24 NKJV).

And when God convicts you of your sins, be honest, confess your sins, and your rebellion, turn from them by the power of God and see the blameless character of God revealed to us through the Scriptures and the Ten Commandments. Believe that Jesus Christ was sacrificed for you on the cross, two thousand years ago, to cleanse you from all your sins so that you may be purified, forgiven, justified and delivered from the bondage of sin. THE TEN COMMANDMENTS were never given to us to deliver us from our sins, but to show us the character of God, so that we can see our own sinfulness; to draw us to Christ so that by faith (See Galatians 5:24) we may have forgiveness by His own blood, the Passover Lamb. By faith in Christ, who was the fulfilment of the sacrificial and ceremonial laws in the Torah (the first five books of the Bible), we can have everlasting hope, forgiveness and life.

The Old Testament laws about purity, diet and sacrifice were temporary enactments for purposes of instruction. They have been cancelled by the New Testament because their symbolic meaning had been fulfilled. They were only *a shadow* of the things to come; Jesus Christ was and is *the substance* of the law (See Colossians 2:14-22).

The moral law of God revealed in the Torah shows us now how we can live lives pleasing to God. The moral law has been rephrased and restated in the New Testament and was upheld by the Lord Jesus Christ and the apostles (Read Ephesians 4-6; Colossians 3; Romans 13:8-10; Matthew 22:36-30; Matthew 5-7 etc.) The moral law will stand for eternity because it shows us the perfections of God, His righteous character, and how God rules the world. He will judge the living and the dead. The moral law and its implication and applications, written in the Torah, have been upheld throughout the New Testament by Jesus Christ and the apostles.

Please look at the Appendixes of how law and gospel correlate to each other and how they lead the sinner to Christ, to be justified by faith.

Yours in Christ
Nico van Zyl
www.interethnicmissions.net

# WHO IS JESUS CHRIST REALLY?

The gospel of John in the Bible describes Jesus Christ in the following ways:

- Jesus is the Word of God who created the universe and became a human being, "In the beginning was the Word, and the Word was with God, and the Word was God. All things were made through Him, and without Him nothing was made that was made.....and the Word became flesh and dwelt among us." (John 1:1-3,14 NKJV).
- Jesus is the Lamb that was slain to take away the sins of the world: "Behold! The Lamb of God who takes away the sin of the world!" (John 1:29 NKJV).
- Jesus is the Bread of Life: "I am the bread of life. He who comes to Me shall never hunger" (John 6:35 NKJV).
- Jesus is the Fountain of Living Water (See also John 7:37-39) "... but whoever drinks of the water that I shall give him will never thirst. But the water that I shall give him will become in him a fountain of water springing up into everlasting life." (John 4:13-14 NKJV) '... and he who believes in Me shall never thirst." (John 6:35 NKJV).
- Jesus is the Light of the world, "I am the light of the world. He who follows Me shall not walk in darkness, but have the light of life." (John 8:12 NKJV).
- Jesus is God "...and the Word was God." (John 1:2 NKJV); "Most assuredly, I say to you, before Abraham was, I AM." (John 8:58 NKJV).
- Jesus is the Good Shepherd. "I am the good shepherd. The good shepherd gives His life for the sheep" (John 10:11 NKJV).
- Jesus is the Door. "Most assuredly I say unto you, I am the door of the sheep.... if anyone enters by Me, he will be saved, and will go in and out and find pasture" (John 10:7,9 NKJV).
- Jesus is the Resurrection and the Life. "I am the resurrection and the life. He who believes in Me, though he may die, he shall

live. And whoever lives and believes in Me shall never die" (John 11:25 NKJV).

- Jesus is the Way, the Truth and the Life: "I am the way, the truth, and the life. No one comes to the Father except through Me" (John 14:6 NKJV).
- Jesus is the True Vine. "I am the true vine and My Father is the vinedresser. I am the vine and you are the branches. He who abides in Me, and I in him, bears much fruit" (John 15:1,5 NKJV).
- Jesus is Eternal Life (See also 1 John 5:11,12; John 3:16) "And this is eternal life, that they may know You, the only true God, and Jesus Christ whom You sent" (John 17:3 NKJV).
- Jesus died and rose from the dead: "For I delivered to you first which I also received: that Christ died for our sins according to the Scriptures, and that He was buried, and rose the third day according to the Scriptures, and that He was seen by Cephas, then by the twelve. After that He was seen by over five hundred brethren at once..." (1 Corinthians 15:3,4 NKJV).
- It is written, "for as many as received Him (Jesus Christ), to them He (God) gave the right to become children of God, to those who believe in His Name" (1 John 1:12 NKJV). God promises the gift of everlasting life to everyone who repents (turns) from their sins and put their trust in Jesus Christ, in His sacrifice on the cross and resurrection from the dead. If you receive Jesus Christ as your Saviour, Lord and Treasure, God the Holy Spirit will come and make His home within you forever. If you receive Jesus for who He is, it proves that you are born from above, born from the Holy Spirit, and are adopted as God's son or daughter (Read John 1:12,13).
- If you reject Jesus Christ in this life as the Saviour and King of the world, and of your life, there remains no way for forgiveness of your sins and no way to escape the horrors and punishment for your sins. You will therefore spend eternity in utter darkness and in hell. We plead with you not to neglect such a great salvation, found in Jesus Christ alone!

Jesus said: "Come to Me all you who labour and are heavily laden, and I will give you rest" (Matthew 11:28 NKJV)

# THE MARVELOUS LOVE OF GOD

In the beginning, when God made the heavens and the earth, God made man with a free will. Tragically, Adam and Eve decided to disobey God. The result was the fall. Since then all people on earth were born with a sinful nature. We have become slaves of sin. But we also choose to sin wilfully. "For all have sinned and fall short of the glory of God" (Romans 3:23 ESV). We are all therefore spiritually dead and separated from God (Read Ephesians 2:1-3). The Bible says that the soul that sins must die and that the wages and penalty of sin are death (Read Rom 6:23). This does not only mean that man must physically die, but that man must die spiritually as well. God's sentence is so severe because He is holy and just and hates all sin. This is the reason why death is in the world. All people die, and every person stands guilty before God because they all have sinned against God. We have told lies. We have stolen things. We have lusted and committed sexual immorality. We have served and worshipped idols. We have blasphemed God's Name and coveted people's possessions. We all stand guilty before God.

But God made a wonderful plan. He promised even from Adam's day that He would make a new way for us to be restored to Himself (See Genesis 3:15). "For God so loved the world, that he gave his only Son, that whoever believes in him should not perish but have eternal life" (John 3:16 ESV). "But God demonstrates His own love toward us, in that while we were still sinners, Christ died for us" (Romans 5:8 NKJV). While we were God's enemies, God sent His Son Jesus Christ to the earth. He lived a sinless life. He did many miracles and at the end of His life, His own people crucified Him on a cross. But even though they sinned in this way against God, Jesus' death was predetermined by God Himself (Read Acts 2). It was God's plan to save many people of their sin. Because the penalty of sin is death, someone had to pay the penalty of death that could release us from sin's punishment. No one's death could take away our sin except the death of One. Jesus Christ, who never sinned, was that One. He alone could take our sin away because He was sinless (Read 2 Cor 5:21) and God in human form.

If we believe that Jesus died in our place as our substitute, to pay for our sins, we will have forgiveness of our sins and we will have everlasting life. The Bible says that, "without the shedding of blood there is no forgiveness of sins" (Read Hebrews 9:22 ESV). That is why Jesus Christ's blood was shed on the cross, outside Jerusalem, about two thousand years ago. All the sacrifices of sheep and goats in the Old Testament were only types and shadows of the real sacrifice that took away the sin of the world.

Three days after Jesus Christ's death, God the Father raised Him from the dead. Now Jesus Christ is sitting at the right hand of the Father. God broke the power of death and the power of the devil. This is the love of God that God demonstrated to the world. The question remains: what is your response going to be to such great love? Are you going to accept and embrace it? Is this love going to rule the course and goals of your life, or are you going to ignore and reject this great love? The choice is yours.

"But as many as received Him, to them He gave the right to become children of God, to those who believe in His name" (John 1:12 NKJV). God is calling you to embrace His love! But as the Bible says, one day Jesus Christ will come on the clouds to judge the living and the dead. If you haven't received Jesus Christ in your life, as your Saviour, and Lord (King), you will be thrown into the lake of fire (See Revelation 20:15). And there all those who have rejected God's Son and His love, will be in torment for all eternity. When God judges the rebellious it will be a display of His justice. God is holy and only those who love Him wholeheartedly will inherit a place in heaven. To love God is in itself a gift; God gives this gift to those who receive the Holy Spirit and it is evidence of a true faith in Christ (See Romans 5:5).

I urge you and beg you, do not let the time of grace pass you by. Listen to God today. God says: "Today, if you will hear His voice, do not harden your hearts" (Hebrews 3:7,8 NKJV).

**Come to God and His love by confessing and turning from your sins.**

## It is finished

These are the greatest and most important words ever uttered in the history of Mankind and they were uttered by the greatest Man that ever lived on planet earth. This Man is Jesus Christ. Not an ordinary Man; not only a Man with high moral standards or merely a prophet. He was God's only begotten Son. He was conceived by the Holy Spirit and born of the virgin Mary. The God-man. Never before and never again will there be a Man like Him. He was one of a kind and came on a mission to this earth. He was without sin. Even though He was tempted in every way while He lived on earth He never gave in to any temptation. Is such a thing possible, you may ask? Yes, it is true. That is why He came and the Bible says it is true (Read Hebrews 2:18; 2 Cor 5:21).

## 'It is finished!'

Jesus said these words at the end of His life; after He was falsely accused of sins that He did not commit. The Roman authorities condemned Him to die on a cross: Pontius Pilate sentenced Him to death at the instigation of the Jewish authorities. He died a criminal's death, although He was no criminal. He was sentenced by the Jews on charges of blasphemy. They said that He claimed to be the Messiah, the Son of God. Jesus said these words as He hung on the cross, as He was suffering and dying. They are the most important words that were ever uttered by any Man.

## It is accomplished

But, what was finished? I will try to sum up the most important points for you although the breadth and height of the meaning of these words have filled volumes of books.

- The price that was paid as a ransom for the sin of believing sinners was paid in full. The punishment for sin was laid on the shoulders of Jesus Christ. He died in the place of believers. The just punishment for sin is death, as revealed in God's Word (See Romans 6:23). We had to die for our sins, but Jesus Christ died in our place, as our substitute, so that you and I can be innocent of sin. There was a divine transaction. Our sins were put on His account on the cross and His righteousness (sinlessness, perfection) was credited to us. Your sin was laid on Him, and His righteousness was put on you (Read Romans 5:6-21). In other words, God will freely forgive and justify believers now on the basis of what Christ has done.

- Jesus broke the power of sin on the cross to set believers free from its rule and power (See Romans 6:6-8; Matthew 1:21).
- God disarmed and defeated principalities and powers, the devil and His angels, making an open spectacle of them and triumphing over them at the cross (Read Colossians 2:15).
- God reconciled (united) believing sinners with Himself at the cross. (See 2 Corinthians 5:17-21) He demolished the enmity between Himself and believers at the cross (See Colossians 1:20).
- God's anger (wrath) and justice towards believing sinners was satisfied by Jesus dying in their place on the cross. God's justice for sin needed to be satisfied, and Jesus met God's requirement: He was God's perfect offering for sin (See Isaiah 53:10). He was God in the flesh who never sinned.

All this Jesus did for those who trust in Christ alone. What Christ accomplished on the cross two thousand years ago, will become a reality in your life only if you truly turn from your sins (your idolatry, adultery, stealing, lies, covetousness, murder, pride, ingratitude, gossip, indifference, slander, drunkenness, dishonouring parents and taking God's Name in vain) and receive Jesus Christ as your personal Saviour and Lord. Have you truly repented of your sins? Have you trusted in Christ for salvation? If you love your sins and the evils of this world and reject Christ, then the wrath of God will abide on you forever!

**It is finished! Is it finished in you?**

*Nico van Zyl*

# THE GLORIES OF GOD'S RIGHTEOUSNESS

One thing is certain. One day all of humankind, all people, men, women and children from all ethnic groups and languages, all who ever lived on planet earth will stand before God's glorious throne and will be judged to an eternity with God's blessing or without it. The judgement seat is set (Read Romans 2:16; Matt 25:31-46, Hebrews 9:27). Man must give an account for the life he or she has lived.

There will be no second chances, no extinction of a human life, no annihilation of a life and no reincarnation. The Bible is clear: Every person is to die once and then the judgement (Read Hebrews 9:27). Another startling and shocking fact is that all mankind need perfection to live before God and to enter His holy place called heaven (See Hebrews 12:14; Isaiah 35:8).

Another tragic fact is that all people who have ever lived, have sinned and they fall short of God's glorious presence. Our own wilful disobedience against God's law and character separates us from the eternal, magnificent God. Our own sins disqualify each one of us from entering His glorious presence. We have made and worshipped idols (real or in our minds), hated people, lied, stolen, cheated, used God's Name in vain and coveted other people and their possessions numerous times. These things God calls sins and we deserve eternal punishment because of our sins. God is holy and just and never overlooks sin. He is of too pure eyes to behold evil!

But wait before you go into despair! Here is the good news: God not only punished our sins in His only Son Jesus Christ, but provided a perfect righteousness whereby we can become perfect in God's eyes! God sent His only begotten Son, Jesus Christ about two thousand years ago and He lived a sinless, perfect life. He obeyed God's law completely and obtained a righteousness whereby God can now justify us. Not only is this true, but He died on a cross in Israel two thousand years ago to pay the penalty for the sins of those who will believe. That's great news!

112

No amount of prayer, good works, shedding of tears or confessions can make us acceptable in God's sight. What we need is God's finished work to be right with Him.

Many people think: Yes, Jesus died in my place as my substitute. He paid the punishment for my sins. He satisfied God's justice and bore the wrath of God for sin and now He demands my obedience so that when I die one day, my works will justify me on judgement day. In other words, Jesus Christ's death was necessary to take away my sins, but now God needs my obedience to the law, (my righteousness) for the final judgement, for justification.

So, some people think, when I die one day I will thank God for His sacrifice but, I rely on my own works to get me into heaven and enjoy His presence.

This position insults God's righteousness and His magnificent grace. Your and my good works (righteousness) do not justify us before God. If we would only sin once we would have a flawed righteousness, an imperfect righteousness, and that would disqualify us on judgement day. We need *perfection*: complete fulfilment of God's law and ONLY JESUS CHRIST obtained that! The only hope for you and me on judgement day is Jesus Christ's blood and righteousness; His substitutionary life and death! We need perfection to be in God's presence and only Jesus Christ obtained righteousness (perfection) because He fulfilled the law of God by His obedience when He lived on this earth.

## REST IN HIS RIGHTEOUSNESS

Stop thinking that God needs your good works to make you right with Him. You need Jesus Christ's perfection, His righteousness, to be accounted (imputed) to you (Read 2 Corinthains 5:21). This happens by faith. Just believe. Accept and embrace this righteousness, and praise God for the life and death of Jesus Christ! Praise Him and thank Him! Receive it as a gift from God. Embrace and receive the most extraordinary and wonderful life of Jesus Christ. "It is accomplished".

"It is finished" were Jesus' words when He died on the cross about two thousand years ago. IT IS FINISHED! Rest in that.

Paul wrote in the book of Romans: "The gospel... is the power of God for salvation to everyone who believes....for in it the righteousness of God is revealed" (Romans 1:16,17 ESV). This is the righteousness of God that we so desperately need.

What would you say if someone gave you ten million dollars as a gift? Would you be happy about it? Would you delight in it? God provided something much more valuable than that! He provided the gift of everlasting life in Jesus Christ to be received by faith. He gives us Himself! He is more valuable than the entire world and the universe put together! All we need to do is receive Him for the Treasure He is. God declares: "For by grace you have been saved through faith. And this is not your own doing; it is the gift of God, not a result of works, so that no one may boast" (Ephesians 2:8,9 ESV).

Let's take hold of His gift and the Giver who is the greatest Gift. Then the good works like confession of sin, prayers, love towards our neighbours and good works will flow naturally and powerfully from you, by the Holy Spirit. A good tree will bear good fruit.

**Let the Foundation of your life be Jesus
Christ, His blood and righteousness.**

# TWO GATES TWO ROADS TWO DESTINIES

Jesus said: "Enter by the narrow gate. For the gate is wide and the way is easy that leads to destruction, and those who enter by it are many. For the gate is narrow and the way is hard that leads to life, and those who find it are few" (Matthew 7:13-14 ESV).

The wide gate represents the world. On this road all religions are right. They say: how can you say Christianity is the only right religion? Who is to judge between right and wrong? The broad road is where a person plays with sin or even where sin is called good. On this road you can steal, lie, smoke, get drunk, listen to what you want, lust after who and what you want, curse who you want, be disrespectful to whom you want and flirt with whom you want. Anything takes the place of the living God: money, sex, television, music, drugs, alcohol, sport, family, computer games, food, success, career, nationality, race or whatever, as long as you can have your idols and God. These things are not necessarily wrong within their God-ordained place, but for many people they dethrone God of His rightful place. We cannot serve idols *and* God at the same time. The broad road is the road where God is dethroned in your heart. This road leads to conscious eternal destruction and suffering away from God's mercy, blessing and love. Most people are on this road and most people will tragically stay on this road according to the Word of God.

The narrow road looks much different. The gate is Jesus Christ (See John 10:7). You cannot enter the narrow road unless Jesus Christ becomes your Treasure. You cannot get onto the road without turning from your sins and idols (Read John 1:12). If you have not received forgiveness from your sins by the blood of Jesus Christ, you will not find yourself on this road. To be on the narrow path means you surrender your whole life to God. When you are on this road you realize Jesus can and will not only be the Saviour of your life, but that He must be Lord as well. If Jesus is not King (Lord) of all in your life, He is not Lord at all in your life. That

115

means He is the rightful Owner and Ruler of your whole life. If He is your Lord (King), then you live in submission to Him and to His body, His people. Then you cannot do as you please. If He is King of your life then He controls your future; how you spend your money; how you spend your time and with whom; what books and magazines you read; what music you listen to; what DVD's you watch; what websites you visit; who your friends are; where you socialize. He then controls the words that come out of your mouth; where you should stay; what job you should do, etc. In short, on this road, in every situation and difficulty you ask: What is your will Lord? Not my will. And when God leads you, you obey. Jesus said, "Not everyone who says to me, 'Lord, Lord,' will enter the kingdom of heaven, but the one who does the will of my Father who is in heaven." (Matthew 7:21 ESV).

This is the narrow road. The narrow road does not mean you never make mistakes or sin, but it does mean that God rules your life and that God saves you from your sinful habits and addictions. On the narrow road, Christ lives within you through the Holy Spirit. On the narrow road, you value what is most valuable: Jesus Christ. On the narrow road, you are willing to suffer tribulation and persecution for the sake of Christ. On the narrow road, you are willing to suffer insults for the sake of Christ. On the narrow road the Bible is precious to you, and rules your life through the Holy Spirit. On the narrow road you delight in the laws of God and esteem the Word of God above your own sinful desires. On the narrow road, you regard the fellowship with the people of God highly, above the company of unbelievers.

The narrow road guarantees eternal happiness and joy and is the only road that leads to heaven. Let's make no mistake: it is a difficult road. It is a road where you sometimes feel you want to quit. Sometimes it is a lonely road. It is a road in the midst of tribulations and suffering, but with God and in God. Humanly speaking it is impossible to get on the road and stay on the road, but Christ said, "... all things are possible with God" (Mark 10:27 ESV).

### Which road are you on?

# IS JESUS CHRIST THE ONLY WAY TO BE SAVED FROM ONE'S SINS AND ENTER HEAVEN?

Is Jesus Christ the only way to God? What about those who have never heard the gospel of Jesus Christ and died? Are they going to hell? Are their sins forgiven in another way? If the Israelites were forgiven for their sins in the Old Testament before Jesus died for the sins of the world, could it be that other people's sins will be forgiven today as well if they have not heard of Jesus Christ? And if that is the case, can we still say Jesus is the *only* way to God?

These difficult questions have puzzled many and led many to conclude that there must be other ways to God as well. But what does the New Testament say about these things? Jesus said, "I am the way, the truth, and the life. No one comes to the Father except through Me" (John 14:6 NKJV). It is written: "Nor is there salvation in any other, for there is no other name under heaven given among men by which we must be saved"(Acts 4:12 NKJV). It is written: "for there is one God and one Mediator between God and men, the Man Christ Jesus who gave Himself a ransom for all" (1 Timothy 2:5). It is written: "...God has given us eternal life and this life is in His Son. He who has the Son has life, he who does not have the Son of God does not have life" (1 John 5:11,12 NKJV).

In these passages of the New Testament (and there are others) God has made it clear that Jesus Christ is the **only** way to receive eternal life. He is the only way to the Father. There is salvation in no one else. He is the only Mediator between God and man. He is the only one who died for the sins of the world and who bore God's wrath because of our sins (See 1 John 2:1,2). Never was there a Man like Him. He was without sin (Read 2 Cor: 5:21); God in the flesh (See John 1:1-3,14). You may ask what about those who never heard the gospel and those in the Old Testament who only had the promises of a coming Saviour?

In the Old Testament people were saved based on the promise of the coming Saviour and the blood (death) of sheep and goats were only types and shadows of the real blood of Jesus that would take away sins. They were saved based on the promises of God and the Christ that would die because of their sins. They **believed** these promises. God credited this to them as righteousness, on the ground of their **faith** in Him who promised (see Genesis 15:6 and the example of Abraham, as well as Hebrews chp. 11).

But what about those who never heard the gospel? If you have time, read the letter of Romans, Chapters 1-3. That will give you an in-depth view of the matter. All we can say of those people who did not have a promise of the Saviour and who died without hearing the gospel is that God is just, holy and loving. God will see to it. We do not know.

What we **do** know is this, "these times of ignorance God has overlooked, but now commands all men everywhere to repent, because He has appointed a day on which He will judge the world in righteousness by the Man whom He has ordained. He has given assurance of this to all by raising Him from the dead" (Acts 17:30,31 NKJV). Jesus said, "Go into all the world and preach the gospel to every creature" (Mark 16:15 NKJV).

Why should we preach the gospel to every person? We should because there is no other way to heaven. We should because God commands it. We should because God has overlooked the times of ignorance when people served other gods, but NOW God has ordained a Man by whom we will be saved if we believe in Him (Read John 3:16.) No one will go to hell because he/she did not hear about Jesus, they will go to hell because of unrepentant sin, because of wilful, continual rebellion against a God who loved them, whom they rejected (See Romans 1,2). People go to hell because they hate God and His laws! They will be sentenced to go to hell because they stand guilty before God on charges of treason against the King of the Universe.

Do we have any warrant NOW to believe that people will go to heaven without embracing Jesus Christ as Saviour and Lord? We do not have a warrant from the New Testament. God commands His followers to "preach the gospel" (Mark 16:15 NKJV) to every person, to witness about Him "to the end of the earth" (Acts 1:8 NKJV), to make disciples of all ethnic groups (Read Matthew 28:18-20). What about you Friend? Are you involved in praying to God and witnessing for God to see His enterprise fulfilled? More importantly: Are we part of that band of followers who worship the Lamb, who are saved from our sins? Are we amongst those whose names are written in the Lamb's Book of Life? (Read Revelation 20:15). Are you?

Woe to us, if we are saved from our sins, but saved for comfort, ease, and indifference to the lost (Read Revelation 3:14-18). May God get us out of our comfort zones; let us be busy fulfilling His Great Commission, going into all the world, spreading the good news, until the last trumpet sounds (See 1 Cor. 15:50-54). May He find our lamps burning bright, filled with the Holy Spirit and faith awaiting the Bridegroom.

Jesus said: "Whoever confesses Me before men, him I will also confess before My Father who is in heaven. But whoever denies Me before men, him I will also deny before My Father who is in heaven" (Matthew 10:32,33 NKJV). May God help us.

**"And I am sure of this, that he who began a good work in you will bring it to completion at the day of Jesus Christ." (Philippians 1:6 ESV)**

# BIBLIOGRAPHY AND RECOMMENDED RESOURCES

- Comfort, Ray, * "The School of Biblical Evangelism"
- Comfort, Ray, * "The Way of the Master"
- Hammond, Peter, * "Biblical Principles for Africa"
- Hammond, Peter, * "The Ten Commandments"
- Hammond, Peter, * "The Greatest Century of Missions"
- Ursinus, Zacharias, * "The Heidelberg Catechism"
- The Oxford Dictionary
- Thomas Watson, * "The Ten Commandments"
- Piper, John, * "Future Justification"
- Piper, John, * "The Passion of Jesus Christ"
- Piper, John, * "God is the gospel"
- Piper, John, * "The Pleasures of God"
- Piper, John, * "Desiring God"
- Mark Dever, * "Nine Marks of a Healthy Church"
- RC Sproul, * "Essential Truths of the Christian Faith"
- RC Sproul, * "What is Reformed Theology?"
- RC Sproul, * "Can I trust the Bible"
- RC Sproul, * "How can I be right with God"
- The Reformation Study Bible, RC Sproul – General Editor
- RB Kuiper, * "God Centered Evangelism"
- John MacArthur, * "The Gospel according to Jesus"
- John MacArthur, * "Saved beyond a Doubt"
- James Kennedy, * "Truth that Transforms"
- Brain Edwards, * "The Ten Commandments for Today"
- John Bunyan, * "Pilgrims Progress"

- Grudem, Wayne, * "Systematic Theology"
- Louis Berkhof, * "Systematic Theology"
- Waldron, Samuel, * "A modern Exposition of the 1689 Baptist Confession of faith"
- Johnstone, Patrick, * "The Future of the Global Church"
- Jason Mandryk, * "Operation World"
- Johnstone, Patrick, * "Serving God in today's cities"